LIVING STUDIES
is a series of high quality
Christian books, both timely
and relevant to today's
problems and challenges. □ In addition to
being some of the best in Christian reading, books in the LIVING STUDIES SERIES
have a dual purpose, being specially designed for small group Bible studies, mid-
week services, adult vacation Bible school,
or as adult Sunday school elective studies.
□ A separate Leader's Guide, designed for
easy out-of-class preparation, makes any lay
person into an interesting and capable dis-
cussion leader. Books and Leader's Guides
(some for six sessions, most for thirteen sessions) are available at your Christian book-
store or write Tyndale House Publishers,
Box 80, Wheaton IL 60189.

HOW COME IT'S TAKING ME SO LONG?

Lane Adams

LS LIVING STUDIES
Tyndale House Publishers, Inc. Wheaton, Illinois

The author gratefully acknowledges permission to
quote from the following versions of the Bible, in
addition to the King James Version:
The Living Bible
© 1971 by Tyndale House Publishers, Inc.,
Wheaton, Illinois.
*The Modern Language Bible, The Berkeley
Version*
edited by Gerrit Verkuyl, Ph.D., © 1945, 1959, ©
1969 by The Zondervan Publishing House, Grand
Rapids, Michigan.
The Revised Standard Version
© 1946 and 1952, Division of Christian Education
of the National Council of the Churches of Christ in
the United States of America, New York, N.Y.
The New American Standard Bible
© 1960, 1962, 1963, 1968, 1971, The Lockman
Foundation, La Habra, California.
The New Testament in Modern English
by J. B. Phillips, © 1958, 1959, 1960 by J. B.
Phillips, The Macmillan Company, New York, N.Y.

Second printing, Living Studies edition, May 1986

Library of Congress Catalog Card Number 84-52187
ISBN 0-8423-1491-1

CONTENTS

FOREWORD

I CAN REMEMBER the radiance I saw on his face and the excitement he expressed. The man was a seasoned Elder of our Hollywood Church. He had given his life to Christ years before and had struggled to grow to become a mature Christian. Discouraging battles with his own humanity had made the Christian life a disappointing experience of ups and downs. Now he had found a liberating secret which gave him hope. He had attended Lane Adams's Inquirers' Group for prospective members of our church. What Lane had shared had given him an exuberant burst of enthusiasm and freedom. He had gone to the classes as a dutiful Elder to be supportive of our church's ministry of evangelism. By the time the course was completed he was not only evangelized himself, he was emancipated from deadly dicta which had locked him on dead center.

I will never forget what this Elder, a Christian for twenty-three years, said to me. "Why did I have to wait so long to discover what Lane taught about the true nature of Christian growth? When I think of all the years of anguishing trial and error, I wish I had learned this twenty-three years ago. Everyone's got to go to those classes!"

What this Elder heard from Lane is the essential content of this exciting book you are about to read. Each time we receive a group of new members, I hear and see the implications of this same inspiration expressed by this Elder. The Session meets with these new members to affirm and encourage their commitment to Christ and their desire to grow in Christ by participation in the adventuresome new chapter of the Book of Acts which is being dramatized in our church. I am always

gratified by the authentic introduction to Christ
Lane has enabled in each of them. But my joy
overflows each time the new members talk about the
vision and vitality they have received about what
it means to grow to maturity in Christ. So many
of the hang-ups and false expectations which I find
in Christians all around the world have been
anticipated and alleviated in these new Christians
uniting with our church.

Lane Adams is obstetrician, pediatrician, and
internist when it comes to introducing people to Christ,
enabling their first stumbling steps of growth
and diagnosing and treating the complex problems
of being faithful and obedient to Christ as maturing
Christians. Few Christian leaders have all these
gifts. But Lane has exercised all of them in his
winsome leadership in our church and now in this
desperately needed book.

I remember when I first met this fellow-adventurer
face to face. We had agreed to meet in Denver
to talk about the possibility of teaming together.
There was that immediate koinonia which is
experienced by two brothers whose hearts feel the
drumbeat of the Master. The same openness,
vulnerability, and honest freedom you will feel on
every page of this book was what impressed me so
much at that first meeting. The usual tension of job
interviews was completely lacking as we shared
our lives with each other. Lane led not from
strength and adequacy but from weakness and a
voracious desire to grow in Christ. I have met few
people whose commitment to Christ was more
stable and yet whose openness about their own needs
was more viable.

It was at that meeting that I first heard the basic
thesis of this book. I had asked Lane what he

wanted to have happen to people through his ministry. In response he outlined the undergirding theory of his ministry of introducing people to the Savior in such a way that they would be free to grow and discover the amazing possibilities of Christ liberated from the reservations and self-justifications which debilitate so many defeated Christians. I still remember the diagram of the invasion, beachhead, and penetration of the enemy-held territory he drew for me. From the experience he had had as a navy pilot in World War II, he illustrated one of the most vivid explanations of conversion and sanctification I had ever heard. I know you will feel the same way as you are drawn magnetically on through the evolving discovery of this thought-provoking book.

I have just finished reading the manuscript for myself. I was personally helped and encouraged by it. So many Christian writers have a way of taking the dynamic of the gospel and complicating it unnecessarily with restrictive rhetoric. Too seldom do we feel the author's own experience of the truth he is communicating. Not so with this book! The thought is profound, but the joy and freedom with which Lane writes pulls the reader on chapter to chapter. This book is like a conversation. The real man who wrote it sparkles through each page. His rich humor, his extensive experience and his Holy Spirit-inspired insights make this book difficult to put down. There is a powerful use of Scripture which reveals Lane's love and understanding of the Bible. The deeply personal illustrations help us to know that the author has lived what he writes. The personal needs in his own life which brought him to ask the basic question of the title, *How Come It's Taking Me So Long to Get Better?* are brewing beneath the surface of so many Christians. This book answers the questions we are all asking. There is nothing more absurd than an answer to an unasked question and nothing more powerful than the clear answer to the deepest questions in our hearts. Here is the answer to one of the most persistent questions I hear asked in so many ways by so many Christians. Lane is a man who has had the courage to say it as it is! I thank God for that.

We have needed this book for a long time but God's timing is always right. There has never been a greater need than now.

I pray that this book will mean to you as much as its author has come to mean to me and our church in Hollywood.

LLOYD JOHN OGILVIE
Pastor, The First Presbyterian Church of Hollywood

PREFACE

"OH! THAT DOES MAKE ME FEEL much
better about a lot of things!"

A young lady said that to me just after I had briefly
reviewed for her the major ideas of this book.
I turned to Virginia Muir, Tyndale House's senior
book editor, who was seated at the same luncheon
table, and said, "If the book brings that kind of
response from its readers, it will have accomplished the
purpose for which it was written."

The young lady who had given the positive
response was a Christian worker who had returned
from an overseas mission field and was presently
engaged in a professional position not related
to institutional Christianity. Happy with her new
vocation, she was obviously still working through the
personal needs which had necessitated her return.

The purpose of this book is to bring comfort
and understanding to all who name Jesus as Lord and
Savior. I pray that its message will free many
believers to patiently enjoy the maturing process
as God is working in their lives. It is designed to
bring a fresh biblical understanding of conversion and
growth, and thereby to bring relief to the person
who keeps wondering, "How come it's taking me
so long to get better?" Since this book concerns
the passage of time, it might be well to point out that
the struggles described here cover a span of
more than twenty-five years.

I wish to acknowledge with gratitude the editorial
assistance of my son-in-law, Terry Moore, and the
exceptionally patient and encouraging secretarial
assistance of Belva Jean Russell. Also, a hearty thanks
to volunteer typists Deena Putnam, Peggy Duarte,
Barbara Kefauver, and Joyce Nelson, who
spent much time transcribing tapes.

LANE G. ADAMS

1

How Come It's Taking Me So Long to Get Better?

THAT SICK FEELING in the pit of my stomach, a mixture of hot anger and bewilderment, told me clearly that I had blown it again. As rapidly as my mind tried to justify my side of the argument, just as rapidly something else deep inside me shrieked "failure"! Another argument with my wife—harsh words, angry voices, accusations, and counteraccusations—arguing about the arguing —endless hurt, given and taken—and now the sullen silence with the swollen feeling of bursting rage.

Each time this recurring agony took place, our differences seemed more impossible to reconcile. A glimmer of hope in one area of the relationship would soon be shattered by deterioration in another.

As bad as all of this was, it wasn't the worst hurt, or the greatest confusion. That came because I was a minister of the gospel of Jesus Christ, and pastor of a wonderful band of Christian people, most of whom had come to believe in Jesus Christ because of me. I was the one who had told, and was telling, them that the living Jesus could heal their wounds and solve their problems. Moreover, I often had counseled them successfully in their marital difficulties without being able to solve my own.

I could cite verse after verse from the Bible, and my seminary training had given me gobs of information on the saving power of Jesus Christ, yet most of it seemed so ineffective in resolving my own difficulty. To make matters more bewildering, while a senior in seminary, I had been honored by Billy Graham with an invitation to join his Team for the first great New York Crusade in 1957. Because of that six-month experience I now had a reputation to live up to.

There were other areas of failure, though none

quite so threatening as the marriage difficulties. My own ego needs drove me compulsively in my work. Just serving God faithfully was not enough. I had to be leading the pack or, at the least, promising to lead the pack in time. Somewhere along the line, to make matters worse, I had equated church work as being the measure of my love for God. Successful church work equals big love for God. Keep so busy, give so much of your time, be available to everybody everywhere, accept every speaking opportunity, and do that to such an extent that just everybody will marvel at how dedicated you are. When they begin to express concerns for your health you know you're really impressing them. A friend once told me, "If a man is on fire for Christ, people will come if for no other reason than to watch him burn!" I needed the approval and attention of others so much that my compulsive activity was about to send me up in smoke. Educational deficiencies and my bizarre background (Navy fighter pilot, nightclub singer, and hotel manager, with a fling at banking and the auto business) drove me to feel I had to prove myself. Wife and child were usually given the short end of the stick in both time and quality of atten- tion. In my blindness I usually interpreted any protest from them as an attack from the devil. So, the ego problem was feeding the marital difficulty.

As spiritual successes mounted in the church, personal failures were facing me with a searing question. In the light of everything I so strongly believed about Jesus Christ and had so dogmatically preached to my people, *Why, oh why, was it taking me so long to get better?* I would often get terrifying glimpses of where I was wrong. I would pray desperately about them, but progress was almost nonexistent so far as I could see.

At times I would begin to doubt that I had come into a saving relationship with Jesus Christ. The reason for this was obvious. All of my brief Christian life I had heard preacher after preacher shout, "If any man be in Christ he is a *new* creature, old things have passed away; behold, all things have become new!"[1] True, there had been a number of things that were new in my life and impossible to explain apart from Jesus Christ. There were also some old things that had passed away, but there were so many other old things in me that just wouldn't seem to die. Covered with a spiritual veneer, but still painfully known to me, their continued presence was a humiliation. Add to this the preaching and teaching which implies that every Christian should *always* exhibit the lofty, positive virtues of "love, joy, peace, longsuffering, gentleness, goodness, faith"[2] and you'll understand why I found myself near to despair.

The revolutionary change which had taken place in the Apostle Paul, plus the glowing testimonies of others about their contemporary experience left me confused over the sadly divided house in which I lived. I was divided as a man and as a husband. Neither problem responded to the crash programs I occasionally employed to alleviate the pressure. In both cases these efforts would often backfire and leave me deeper in despair. The more bravely I plunged on in my work, the greater my sense of hypocrisy.

At that time of my life and in my circle of friends there seemed to be just no one else who was plagued with my kind of problems. If they had them, they were as silent about them as I was. I lived in fear that someone would find out, yet I longed for some understanding, warm-blooded human to know how I hurt. In short, I had become a prisoner of the very problem that lay at the heart of my difficulties with my wife—no communication—not with her nor with anyone else—not at a deep and honest feeling level. All of this was hid from me at the time. (Only 20-20 hindsight has made it possible for me to see it, even now.)

In this struggle I often sought the counsel of others by reading books, and by veiled and round-about questioning of men that I admired. Never admitting to the real specifics, I yet longed to know more about what brought maturity in the Christian life because it was becoming obvious to me that I didn't have it. (Oh! How hard it was for me to face and admit this to myself!) There was general agreement on what brought maturity. Serious, in-depth, daily study of the Bible; a living relationship to God in prayer; regular sharing of your faith in Christ through witness; involvement in the local church and other service to mankind as opportunities presented themselves. All of this I had been doing for several years. Why were the results not greater?

This introduced the subject of time; so, from then on, my questions would also revolve around the subject of how long it takes to become mature. Bear in mind an important thing implicit in theological education. *It takes three years* (*usually*) *to graduate from seminary.* At that point it is assumed that you are mature enough to provide spiritual leadership to a congregation of people, many of whom have lived much longer than you have, and have known God much longer than you have. So, whether anyone actually came out and said it, the implication was that three intensive years of study and practical preparation would make one mature enough to be a spiritual leader. I had already had that, plus other learning opportunities which few others were privileged to experience. Yet, my problems were about to sink me.

To this question, of "How long does it take to mature spiritually?" I received almost no help at all from others. Answers ranged anywhere from a concept of conversion that presupposed maturity arriving overnight to an honest "I don't know." But even those who said they didn't know seemed to presume that it shouldn't take too long. Because none of us were really dealing with, or even admitting to, the specifics of our problems, we would retreat to Bible verse clichés and just keep on, hoping for the best.

But the pain of my own personal difficulties forced me to think, pray, and search for some insights that would relieve the building tension. But always the question was rising up inside me, *"How come it's taking me so long to get better?"*

2

The Great Invasion

INVASION! The word held a strange fascination for me. Not so much in the military sense as in the sense of what happened to a person at the time of his conversion. I had come to realize that when a person's faith led him to receive Jesus as Lord and Savior he was actually invaded by the same Spirit that had raised Jesus from the dead. Moreover, I really believed that was what had happened to me. There was ample evidence for it. I had changed. My questions were, "Why hadn't I changed more?", "How come it's taking so long?", and "Why do I still have such a problem with temptation and sin?" So you're invaded by the Spirit of Jesus. What happens then?

One day while thinking about this I went back in my mind to my Navy days in WW II. I took out pencil and paper, drew an imaginary island and relived the process of invading an enemy-held island. What I discovered changed my life.

In the Pacific during the early part of WW II the United States and her allies quickly lost their possessions island by island. An island-hopping technique was devised to regain the Pacific in order to protect Hawaii, Alaska, and California from an expected invasion by the Japanese.

Each enemy-held island was very carefully photographed and strategically considered to see whether or not it was important enough to be retaken. Some were bypassed. Others had to be recaptured if we were to regain the Pacific. These islands were photographed in great detail by aerial reconnaissance to locate the fortifications. Then would begin a very meticulous softening-up process against the enemy-held island. Headquarters would examine the photographs and begin an aerial assault using rockets, bombs, and strafing to knock out those areas of known strength. Several areas of the island would be targets so that the exact place of invasion would not be revealed. After we in the aircraft had done everything we could, the big ships with the more accurate long-range guns would begin pinpoint shelling from off-shore. The object of this process was sufficiently to weaken the fortifications so when the troops landed they would be able to secure beachheads.

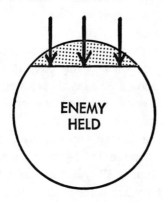

Then the climactic moment would come when the troop ships would deploy their precious human cargo, the United States Marines. And the Marines, having boarded their small landing craft, would rendezvous and assault the beach. By prearrangement they would come onto the beach at a particular place and secure a beachhead. This would be merely a fragment of the island because they did not want to take more than they had the troops to hold. They would dig in, controlling that beachhead, and then very confidently radio back to combat information center saying, "The Marines have landed, and the situation is well in hand." Now, anyone with an eyeball for real estate can tell you that this was quite a presumption on the part of the Marines, because they

held such a small beachhead on the island, and
the enemy, with all his genius, held all the rest.
No matter how badly he was battered, inevitably the surface of the enemy's defenses had hardly
been scratched when the men assaulted the
beach. (Anyone who was in Iwo Jima or Gua-
dalcanal knows what that means.)

Now notice something about those Marines:
Never in the course of the war in the Pacific
were they pushed off an island. So, although it was
arrogant presumptuousness for them to radio back,
"Marines have landed, the situation is well in hand,"
the truth was that the situation *was* well in hand,
even though they only held a tiny piece of the
total island. As soon as the beachhead was secured
other craft would come and land heavier
equipment, such as tanks and artillery.

All this time the softening-up process continued
along the front, because the Marines never intended
to remain on the beach. They had not come for
a beach party. They had come to drive to the very
heart of the island eventually. When the situation
on the beachhead was secure and enough of the
heavy stuff was safely on the beach, they
would launch an offensive. Their intention was
to bite off another hunk of enemy-held territory,
secure it, then take another hunk, secure it, and
so on until the entire island was captured. About
the time they secured one piece there would be
another massive drive into another area to take
more of the island. This process would continue
until the entire island would become the possession
of the United States.

Why am I telling you this? Because I have just
drawn what is for me the most helpful picture of
Christian conversion and the Christian life that
I've seen. We are all islands of self in the hands

of the enemy. Conversion is like an invasion and the Christian life is like a war.

When we respond to the invitation of Jesus, "Behold, I stand at the door, and knock; if any man hear my voice, and open the door, I will come in to him, and will sup with him, and he with me,"[1] then the Holy Spirit of Christ invades us and establishes a beachhead in our lives. An enemy-held island now has inside it the invading force of our friendly God. He is beginning a conquest by love, not by tyranny, but we must always remember it is just a beginning.

There is a sincere but mistaken form of evangelism which gives the impression that the total conquest of the island is accomplished by the mere invasion. Both the Bible and human experience deny that this is the case, yet such notions persist, and when they are believed by the new Christian he is being set up for an agonizing experience in the not too distant future. The realities of life with the continual sin problem still staring him in the face will finally lead him to deny that reality, or he must assume there is something faulty with his conversion. Some begin to wonder if they are converted at all.

The important thing to see is that the initial reception of Jesus Christ brings an invasion of the human personality by God himself. John 1:12 says, "But as many as received him, to them gave he the power to become the sons of God. . . ." The beachhead God establishes is the beginning and that is instantaneous. The battle for the island called "you" is the long-range process of maturing.

In the Old Testament the Holy Spirit seems to have provided an external influence on a select few, while in the New Testament Jesus promises that the Holy Spirit will be internal, within the believer's body.[2] In the Old Testament even that external influence of the Holy Spirit might be withdrawn as in the cases of King Saul and Samson. In Psalm 51 David evidenced fear that the Holy Spirit might be taken from him. However, Jesus clearly states, "If you love me, obey me; and I will ask the Father and he will give you another Comforter, and *he will never leave you.*"[3]

So invasion is an apt word to describe what happens at the beginning of the Christian life—but the invasion only produces a beachhead.

But before the beachhead can be established there must come the softening-up process.

3

The Softening-up Process

IN EFFECT the Bible says we are each
an enemy-held island. We are isolated and sep-
arated from God and others by a sea of sin, fear,
and insecurity, and are dominated by self-centered
urges that make us say, with the Apostle Paul, "My
own behavior baffles me."[1] Separation from
one another is the effect of our greater separation
from God. The prophet Isaiah said, ". . . .but your
iniquities have made a separation between
you and your God, and your sins have hid his
face from you so that he does not hear."[2] Because
of this all of us tend to be like the man whose
wife said, "My husband is like a mysterious
island. I feel as though I've been circling in a
little boat for twenty years, and never invited to
land." It is only when we weary of this lonely
island-like life that we begin to think of an alternative.
It is the consequence of our sin that finally
makes the pain of the isolation more than we can
bear.

The softening-up process that precedes Christian
conversion can take one of a hundred forms. Generally it involves a crisis of some sort brought on
by the consequence of our own sin. There are occasions, however, where a tragedy that has no
direct connection with our sin presents us with a
situation we can't handle without God. I have seen
people brought to the end of themselves in a
multiplicity of ways. The "softening-up" process in
my own case was hastened by marital disaster
and a lack of vocational direction. I've seen
others "softened up" by economic distress, al-
coholism, sexual problems, career disappointments,
political fear, drug addiction, absence of life
purpose, shattering guilt, prison terms, ruptured relationships, consuming hate, and even disillusion-

ment over success. Others have been "softened up"
by the death of a loved one, while others have
been touched by merely observing the transformation
of another person being invaded by Jesus Christ.
The different things that soften people up to the
great invasion of God are as diverse as people
and are as unique and original as God himself.

But whatever the crisis or situation that brings
the process to a head, it is usually characterized by
the individual's becoming aware of two things:
that there is something too big for him to handle
by himself; and that the God who directs this uni-
verse actually loves him and wants to take over
his life and handle it for him. It is then that
the admission that one is an enemy-held island will
bring the invasion of the Holy Spirit. Jesus said,
"Behold, I stand at the door and knock, and if anyone will hear my voice and open the door, I will
come in to him. . . ."[3] For some of us a mere knock
by the Lord was not enough. It was more like, "Behold, I stand at the door and bomb . . ." before
we softened up to the point of seeing our need and
God's sweet answer in Jesus. Nevertheless, better
a Divine bomb than a continuation of our lives
under the domination of a totalitarian devil.

So we saw our need and prayed that sweet prayer
of new beginnings, "Come into my heart, Lord Jesus; make my heart your home!"

But then, what should one expect to have happen
once he's prayed that prayer? So many testimonies would lead you to believe that all the old
junk was gone overnight and that every little old
thing became brand new just as quickly. It just
didn't happen like that to me, as bravely as I tried
outwardly to maintain that it did. The baby Christian
wants so to please his new family that he's apt
to play the game of "pretend" about his new life

just to get the affirming response from his brothers and sisters. If he isn't told honestly what to expect, then his big mouth may lead him into the trap of spiritual hypocrisy. At the beginning it will all feel so good he may be quite a while realizing that his life doesn't really square with what his flapping lips insist.

Further confusion was added to my situation. It was marital discord which brought my wife to the point of suggesting that we read the New Testament looking for answers. It was during this time that Jesus became a living power in my life. He started the process of change in me, and many of our difficulties began to look far less threatening. Therefore, in my early efforts to share my new faith I would announce dramatically that Christ had saved our marriage. Now that was true, but you can imagine the confusion that followed when we continued to have difficulties. Because of where my public mouth was I tried to ignore those private problems in hopes they would just go away. Annette tried to help me face them but I found it nearly impossible to admit their seriousness, much less really deal with them. How could I admit to them when I had so often implied that my conversion had taken away those difficulties? Wouldn't this put Jesus Christ in a bad light? Wouldn't that be a lack of faith in his power to meet those problems? You can almost guess the next step, can't you? Sure! I put all the blame on my wife, and stupidly told her so. You can be quite sure that solved nothing. It only made matters worse, and understandably so.

What should receiving Jesus Christ do for me? Discernible growth makes things bearable. But, when things aren't getting any better, and are actually getting worse, hope begins to fade and doubt begins to creep in. My good brother Lloyd Ogilvie says, "Discouragement is the illegitimate child of false expectations!"—and I was discouraged. My expectations had been false because I had not fully understood what had happened to me.

4

The Beachhead

JESUS CHRIST had captured a small beach-head in me in spite of the fact that I had "totally surrendered" my life to him. He had given me all of himself, but I could only give him as much of me as I knew and understood. There was so much of me that was hidden from my conscious awareness. He knew all about it but I didn't, and it would seem that Christ only goes where he is invited in a life. Because the data in that hidden part of my life was painful I had shoved it away from my own awareness. Moreover, I didn't want to face that part of me because of the pain it would bring. In a sense I wanted him to cure me of things that I was unwilling to admit were a problem. "Make me right, Lord, but don't ask me really to face what's wrong!" was often my attitude.

There were also things that I was *incapable* of facing at that time. The full and complete knowledge of those things all at once would have shattered me. But God in his mercy wanted me to face only so much as I could bear and deal with in a wholesome way.

God's Spirit had occupied a beachhead in my life. Where his forces were dug in there was love, joy, peace, longsuffering, gentleness, goodness, faith, meekness, temperance. But there was a great gob of me that wasn't occupied by anything other than my old sinful nature.

Usually, right after a conversion experience there is a period of pure, blissful peace *and I had it*. The joys of forgiveness, eternal life, and the love of Jesus swelled my heart to bursting. It was as though the forces of the old corrupt part of me had been shocked into quiet acceptance of the invasion of God.

Then there was that day when the peace and

quiet of my beatific beachhead began to shake with
the rumble of tanks, followed by the thump of
an artillery barrage as my own personal forces
of hell began a screaming counterattack on
God's beachhead. It was terrifying! Somehow,
somewhere, I had gained the impression that my
conversion to Jesus had laid all of those rotten
impulses to rest. Yet, here they were raging at
me with intensified fury.

As fearful as those things were, an ever greater
fear was that somehow the Lord had departed from
me. The guilt which accompanied the resur-
gence of evil impulses made me wonder if he had
just given up on me. I felt he would surely be justi-
fied in doing so. After all I was such a disappointment to *me,* what must I be to him? It was
a bewildering and frightening experience. At
times the misery was so intense that I was sure that
the only solution was to throw in the towel and give
up on the whole idea of being a Christian.
There were times when I tried to do just that. The
trouble was I had come to know the *truth* in
Jesus Christ and it no longer seemed that I had
the power to ditch him. *The fact* of him would not
go away, and somehow the light of that *fact* still
illuminated my way, even in the midst of self-
created darkness. Caught in such a dilemma I would
confess my sins to him, half-believing that it would
do no good and half-longing for that sweet
touch of his forgiveness. Of course, the
latter would be my experience, and in the joy of
another new beginning I would rush to promise him
all manner of perfection in the future to make up
for the past. That had built-in failure at the
heart of it because I was still not facing that unconquered part of my island that was ruled by my
old nature.

Just as I was penning that last sentence my
phone rang and I heard the voice of a friend I
had not heard from in eight years. My last
contact with him had been during a Crusade in his
home town. As a disc jockey he had inter-
viewed me on the air and had listened while I
had fielded telephoned questions from his fans, most
of whom were teen-agers. However, neither my
best efforts at witnessing to him, nor our
growing friendship had brought him a step closer to
any kind of commitment to Christ. But on the oc-
casion of this call he brought to me the exciting
news that he had come into a fantastic experience
with Jesus Christ. "Man," he said, "I just gotta talk
to you!"

When we got together he related a series of experiences with the living Christ that could only
be described as startling and overwhelming. During
this time he had also become an avid student of
the Bible. He had experienced some truly amazing
and ecstatic revelations of the living Christ.
The problem was that these gigantic experiences
had become less and less frequent, plus the fact
that some of his old evil impulses were once again
pushing at him for fulfillment. He was a living
illustration of what I had just written. The invasion of God had been so spectacular that the forces
of his old nature had been shocked into temporary
quiescence. God had landed, the beachhead was
secured. But when the dust settled he discovered
that the enemy was still present in his island.
Since he had not been led to expect this, serious questions about the validity of his conversion began to
plague him, not to mention some sickening doubts
about his sanity.

I shared with him in sketchy fashion some
of the ideas I'm sharing with you. Relief came

from the realization that he fit the pattern of most Christian people. But it was sobering for him to realize that he was now in for a long war against his entrenched old nature.

By now some of my readers have already begun to think of some Christians they've known that don't seem to fit this pattern of invasion which produces only a small "beachhead." A word of caution and a word of explanation are in order. First, don't ever build your theology on human experience. Our understanding of what God does in us has to come from the Bible first. Conversion experience is valid only in so far as it is confirmed by the Bible. Secondly, the only person we really know about from the inside is ourselves. It has been my experience to observe some new Christians who gave the distinct impression that they were riding a perpetual wave of spiritual victory. There was no hint at all that they were experiencing any of the grinding struggles I had. But when honest sharing by fellow believers finally made them feel safe enough to open up, the same pattern of internal Christian warfare was revealed.

But both the Bible and Christian experience would indicate one thing very clearly which helps to understand the wide difference observed in the impact of conversion on various people. That is the simple fact that the initial size of God's beach-head varies from person to person.

5

How Big Is Your Beachhead?

HOW DO YOU FIGURE IT? Two people
are converted to Christ at the same time. Spiritually
speaking, one takes off like a scalded dog, and
the other is so slow in progress that a turtle looks
like a speed demon in comparison. I've seen
this happen both as an evangelist and as a pastor
The temptation is to leap to a simplistic explanation which may run anywhere from doubting the
sincerity of number 2 convert to an outright
denial that the person is really a Christian. Either
way, number 2 is hurt, not helped, by such an att
tude of judgment, and number 1 may not be able
to handle the heady praise that will come his way
for his performance. Despair grips number 2 and
pride creeps up on number 1.

All of us know that we ought to move toward
maturity, but few of us have ever really sat down
and figured out what it is like, or whether we
or others have arrived there. Too frequently the
standard for Christian maturity amounts to glib verbal expression of the gospel and observance of a
local code of don'ts. The first puts a premium on
how you can tell others the gospel and your own
personal experience. The second puts a premium on
things you're no longer doing that you used to do in
your pre-Christian days. The truth is that many of
us have aone both of these things splendidly and
had lives totally devoid of love. According to
the Savior himself, love is the only standard by
which we may judge whether or not a believer
is truly a believer and on his way toward maturity.

One thing for certain, the babe in Christ is going
to have a hard time mustering even a vague reflection of the love of God in his life, and if someone
applies the standard of maturity to him that is found
in 1 Corinthians 13, it might well come near to

plunging him into a terrible pit of despair
over how far short he falls. I never will forget
how utterly miserable I felt after my first reading
of Henry Drummond's little classic, *The Greatest
Thing in the World.* There's nothing wrong with
a beachhead baby Christian reading a message like
Drummond's if there is somebody there to balance
it off with an understanding that it may take a
good long while for the baby to even begin to
be able to reflect what Drummond is talking about.
That's why it is so crucial that the babe in
Christ understand right from the outset a very
important thing.

That is, that his *position* in the eyes of God
is perfect from the moment he believes and receives
the Savior into his enemy-held island. His *position*
is based on who Jesus Christ is and what he has
done for him. It is only when we are secure in the
knowledge that our *position* is perfect in the sight
of God that we have the courage to either face up
to or admit that our *condition* is miserable. The work
of Jesus Christ was achieving that *position* for us
sinners, and the work of the Holy Spirit is to remedy
our lousy *condition.* Scripture spells this phenome-
nal fact out for us. It says, "For by that one
offering he made forever perfect in the sight of God
all those whom he is making holy."[1]

As a babe in Christ, I was forever plagued
with the distinct impression that my salvation was
going to be withdrawn for nonperformance. I was
quite sure that one day the Lord would simply have
to say to me, "I've been very patient with you,
Lane, but today you went too far and now it's all
over between us!" How much anguish I could
have been saved had I known of the security of
the believer right from the start. I needed to know
that my security was based on what Jesus is and

what he has done, rather than on what I am and what I have done, or for that matter, left undone.

I suppose that as a human being I have been so bound up in manipulative love that is always swapping things that I'm dumbfounded when confronted with a love like that which I can't shut off by my nonperformance. I can still relive the flash of sheer joy that my heart knew when I discovered that ". . . .He guarantees right up to the end that you will be counted free from all sin and guilt on that day when he returns. God will surely do this for you, for he always does just what he says, and he is the one who invited you into this wonderful friendship with his Son, even Christ our Lord."[2] It is only when my heart knows that kind of security that I can honestly face up to how small that beachhead may be that God has in my life. It is only when I rest in that kind of love and that kind of keeping power that I can honestly turn and face how much of the old nature there is in me. But then, that still doesn't answer why the size of individual beachheads varies to such a degree.

We Christians are greatly indebted to psychological research that has been talking for years about the difference between the conscious and the unconscious mind. Some of the early leaders even saw a connection between psychology and religion. Phillip Mairet notes that ". . . .with Jung the psychology of the unconscious merges into the realm of religion. . . ."[3] "The psychiatrist gradually came to the conclusion that, underlying the conflicts and resolutions of the conscious mind, there is an unconscious psyche, of unknown depth, perhaps unfathomably."[4] "Freud too, regarded the unconscious. . . .to be the repository of all the desires, ideas, and memories rejected and repressed by the conscious personality. . . ."[5] The conscious mind would then be that area of our thinking capacity from which we can have immediate recall of all current and considerable past data. The unconscious mind is filled with that data that is too puzzling or painful or disgusting to allow into our conscious awareness. Most would agree that neurotic behavior develops when data in the unconscious mind dictates activities in the conscious realm. Paul's already quoted cry of exasperation about himself is a classic illustration of this, "My own behavior baffles me."[6] The interesting thing about that comment of Paul's is that it was made after Jesus Christ had far more than just a beachhead in his life.

What I'm suggesting is that a person receives Jesus Christ into the conscious part of his being. The size of his beachhead then would be determined by the accuracy with which he can think in reality about himself. I can only give as much of myself as I know and understand to as much of Jesus Christ as I know and understand. This then would account for the varying impact of conversion on different people. It would help to explain why at times a person chinning on the edge of the gutter, who has faced the corruption of his own heart, often makes far more dramatic progress in the Christian life than, say, a person raised in a superreligious atmosphere, who, in his desire to give an outward religious performance, has never really faced some of the deep and ugly things that he has going on inside of him. His religion has demanded that he repress those things and not even begin to face up to their presence in his life. His denial of their reality just shoves them into the basement where they haunt him as a phantasm. When he faces these things with the security of a true believer and the sustaining power of the Holy Spirit, he can then admit them and by the power of God let Christ take over that part of his life as well.

Whenever newspapers or magazines diagram the progress of warfare they inevitably use arrows to indicate new points of aggressive penetration and advance by the opposing forces. Those arrows are an appropriate illustration of the piercing pain often associated with progress in the Christian life. Like the arrow indicating military penetration, the Bible says of itself, "For whatever God says to us is full of living power; it is sharper than the sharpest dagger, cutting swift and deep into our innermost thoughts and desires with all their parts, exposing us for what we really are."[7] In other words the move toward maturity involves the Word of God helping us to expose and face the garbage in our unconscious minds. All we need to do is to confess that that material revealed to us is true, and allow God to cleanse it and occupy the new territory which he has revealed to us. It isn't that God is ignorant of what lies in my unconscious mind. He isn't. "He knows about everyone, everywhere. Everything about us is bare and wide open to the all-seeing eyes of our living God; nothing can be hidden from him to whom we must explain all that we have done."[8] God has always known about all that reprehensible junk in the basement of our lives, the unconscious mind. With perfect timing, he is simply showing us new territory that he needs to occupy by the power of his Holy Spirit. He will never show us more than we can bear at one time.

I used to have growing pains as a kid, but they were nothing compared to the pain of spiritual growth that has come to me as I've been forced to face what I am essentially like in the depth of my being. Again, how kind of God that he has only showed me what I could bear and has patiently waited for me to continue to face up.

Notice something about that little diagram of mine. The more you advance the front line of God's invading force, the broader the front gets. This means that the more we are occupied by God the greater our view is of the corruption that yet remains within us. Could this be why Paul said in Romans 7:18, "I know I am rotten through and through so far as my old sinful nature is concerned. . . ."?[9] That's the same chapter in which he called himself a wretched man, yet when one sees the maturity reflected in the entire document of the book of Romans one can only assume that Paul had risen to a great level of maturity to be able to pen such a document. Has it not also been the testimony of outstanding Christians over the years that the godlier a man was, the more conscious he was of the corruption that yet remained within him? Toward the end of his life Paul still called himself, "the chief of sinners."[10]

God then takes only what we can give him in the way of a beachhead. The problem is not "getting more of God," but letting God "get more of us." The deeper problem is that there is a great section of us with which we are not in touch, in the unconscious mind. Until we get in touch we can't give that part of ourselves to God. Perhaps this is what Paul is talking about when he says, "In my mind I want to be God's willing servant but instead I find myself still enslaved to sin. . . .There is something else deep within me in my lower nature that is at war with my mind and wins the fight and makes me a slave to the

sin that is still within me. So you see how it is; my
new life tells me to do right but the old nature
that is still inside me loves to sin."[11] We can take
comfort in the fact that that which is hidden to us
is revealed to God and that too is already under
the blood of the cross of Jesus Christ. The knowledge
of forgiveness in that area of our lives is applied
when we are enabled by the penetration of the Word
of God and the Holy Spirit to see what is wrong,
admit it, and claim the sweet forgiveness that
has already been made available.

Paul himself may have been on the verge of
some really bad emotional problems when he met
Jesus Christ on the road to Damascus. Consider
his behavior; rigid, dogmatic, and violent, and all under a religious cloak. He assisted in the murder
of Stephen, and I don't think we're demeaning
the Apostle when we say he was in bad shape.

What happens in Christian conversion is
this: the Spirit of God as the Lamp of the Lord
progressively reveals the inner unconscious self. We
get more and more of a revelation of what we're
really like on the inside as the invading force of
God begins to penetrate the unconscious. It's not a
pretty picture that we find, but we are able to face
it because of our *position*. We don't have to put on
unnecessary masks because we are secure. We
can, therefore, be honest and begin to cooperate
with the invading force of God, finding out who we
are, what we are, and what is really going on in
our lives. It might be a very helpful exercise to go
back and think seriously about your ability to
think with accuracy about yourself at the time that
you invited Jesus Christ to invade your life.
You can't know where you are in the Christian
pilgrimage until you know where you started.
You can't get an accurate indication of your

progress unless you know that from which you are progressing. Hold on to your secure *position* in Jesus Christ or you can never bear to be honest about your *condition*.

One of the things that I have discovered in the quarter century that I have known Jesus Christ is that God is much nicer than most of us have imagined. It's so important to see him as a loving and kindly and benevolent heavenly Father. "As a father has compassion for his children, so the Lord tenderly sympathizes with those who revere Him. For He knows what we are made of; He keeps in mind that we are dust."[12]

No matter how big your beachhead was at the time of conversion, it still produced only a spiritual infant with all the obvious needs of an infant. You might even say that at our spiritual birth, regardless of the size of the beachhead, all we ever really amount to is "beachhead babies."

6

Beachhead Babies

CHRISTIANS have habitually demanded too much too soon from spiritual infants, commanding them to conform to patterns of maturity that it may have taken others years and years to attain. For many a "beachhead baby" this pressure is more than they can bear, so they flee from the source of the pressure.

When this happens many church people offer searing judgments on the baby Christian, the evangelist involved, and sometimes call in question the whole idea of evangelism.

If the church represents the spiritually mature, then it follows that it is the responsibility of the mature to relate themselves to the immature. The mature must accommodate themselves to the needs of the immature, and meet them *where* they are and see them for *what* they are.

These new Christians are spiritual infants with all the limitations of infancy. The parent takes care of the young child, particularly in infancy and in the years of dependence. The mature church must assume its role of loving parental responsibility in relation to the spiritual infant.

It is amazing, but true, that the average church will often expect more spiritual maturity from new believers than they will from most of their old-established members. When such maturity is not immediately forthcoming, then criticism is leveled. Certainly this request for a reversal of traditional thinking must be carefully supported by the Word of God.

According to John 3 there is such a thing as spiritual birth. This is not optional; it is necessary if one is to see the Kingdom of God. 1 Peter 2:2 indicates that there is a state of spiritual infancy from which we grow by the intake of the Word of God. Paul indicates in Colossians 1:28 that spiritual growth should culminate finally in spiritual maturity.

There will be little argument about spiritual birth or spiritual maturity, but almost no one seems to take seriously the intermediate stages demanded by the analogy of physical and spiritual life paralleling one another in a developmental process. While avoiding the absurdities inevitably involved in pressing the analogy too far, I do believe that for every stage of physical development there seems to be a corresponding stage of spiritual development.

Thus, in the process of time, utilizing God's appointed means of grace—the Word, prayer and sacraments—the inquirer moves through these various stages: from the nursery to the kindergarten, into the primary and junior stages of life, through the area of agonizing spiritual adolescence, into young adulthood, and finally into maturity.

However, I do not believe that we will be able to appreciate this process of growth until we really come to grips with what we mean by spiritual infancy.

The whole matter is greatly complicated by the chronological confusion that inevitably results when, say, a 40-year-old Ph.D. is at one and the same time a spiritual infant. We relapse into a humanistic process of reasoning which simply will not admit to the fact that all the limitations of infancy are his. We automatically expect and demand too much of him.

Only when we apply the limitations of physical infancy to this new spiritual creature will we see him in the proper light. Only then will we avoid the pitfall of expecting too much too soon.

(Certainly, knowledge acquired prior to conversion can be—and often is—rapidly assimilated in the new Christian framework with much benefit, but just as often it isn't and thus hampers sanctification.)

What is a newborn baby like? What does he do? What do you expect from him? A look at physical infancy will help us to know what to expect of the spiritual infant.

First, the newborn baby has a voracious appetite for a specific kind of food. The trouble is, he can't feed himself. Someone who loves him must feed him. It is pointless to set the table with a banquet and then wonder why he doesn't show up. The food must be brought to him, and the nipple placed in his mouth. So also the babe in Christ. Someone who loves him must feed him with the milk of the Word until he learns to feed himself. The patient parent finally lives to see the babe learn to take care of nourishing himself.

Second, the newborn baby sleeps most of the time. As a new father I remember waking up in the middle of one night because of a strange quietness. No crying! I tiptoed over to the crib to admire my tiny offspring.

While standing there looking at the little form, in the half light, I was gripped with fear as I realized that I could not detect any evidence of breathing. For one moment of panic I contemplated the possibility that she was dead. For all the world she looked like it. Closer examination revealed that she was very much alive, and complaining over being so rudely awakened.

So it is with the babe in Christ. He will seem to be sound asleep so much of the time that you will even begin to wonder if there is any spiritual life there at all. Give him time; he'll wake up.

I recall the sound advice given me once by the late Dr. L. Nelson Bell, when I complained about a lack of evidence of spiritual life in some of my newer church members. He said: "Lane, don't dig up the seed to see if it is growing."

Be patient; the babe in Christ will spend less and less time sleeping as he grows up. Accept the fact of the work of grace *by faith,* and then rejoice when God makes it possible to see the outward evidence of spiritual life.

Third, the newborn baby makes a lot of noise that doesn't make sense to anyone except the parents who love him. This is so often true of the newborn Christian. Tragically, many who are supposed to be mature are quite put off with the utterances of a baby-Christian, and react to them in unloving ways that shock the soul of the infant believer and inhibit his growth.

The super-orthodox are often the most guilty of this, blasting the babe in Christ when he doesn't parrot the party-line with just the right clichés and accepted jargon.

Fourth, the newborn baby exercises almost constantly when he is awake. But most of his exercising consists of meaningless, uncoordinated movements of arms, head, and legs. In brief, he seems to be going off in all directions at once, but he never gets anywhere. But given time and patient encouragement he will learn to get about so well that he'll run a healthy parent ragged just trying to keep up. This is so characteristic of the babe in Christ that it hardly needs further application.

Fifth, the newborn baby is certain to dirty his diaper with astounding regularity. Just as surely the babe in Christ will, through spiritual failures, do the same thing. Nothing tests the genuineness of the spiritual parents' love more than this. Having had an unrealistic expectation of the infant believer they are mortified that his failure has caused embarrassment to them.

I remember the times when we showed our baby girl off for the first time to relatives or friends. Eager to impress them with her outstanding qualities, we would bathe and dress her to look like the picture on a pablum box. On several occasions like this at the crucial moment of presentation she managed an odor so overwhelming that even her parents found it hard to smile or be enthusiastic. There was nothing wrong with the timing of her infantile functions. We were just expecting too much from a baby.

Spiritual pride is often so damaged by the failure of a spiritual offspring that the infant is disowned and responsibility for his actions is disavowed. The Christian who would treat a spiritual babe in this way had better hope that his Savior will not treat him in the same fashion.

To his own spiritual infants Jesus said, "Now you are clean through the Word which I have spoken unto you."[1] We need to be ever present with the cleansing Word for the stumbling babe.

We must remind the babe over and over again that the initial love of Christ came to him in spite of what he was, and that the continuing love of Christ will come to him in spite of what he is, and never because he has merited it with perfect conduct. "If we say that we have no sin, we deceive ourselves, and the truth is not in us. If we confess our sins he is faithful and just to forgive us our sins, and to cleanse us from all unrighteousness."[2]

We must warn the babe against expecting too much of himself, while guarding him against complacency about the evil that is within him. He must be reassured again and again that "if any man sin, we have an advocate with the Father, Jesus Christ the righteous."[3]

He must not only sense the forgiveness of God,

but also of God's servant. Often the babe will be able to sense the unconditional love of God through another Christian before he will be able to sense it directly from God.

Above all else the babe in Christ will respond to the unconditional love of Christ as it is expressed to him by another Christian, one who is willing to accept him as he is with all of his infancy showing, one who is willing to encourage even the slightest indication of progress, and who knowingly understands and accepts the inabilities, weaknesses, and failures.

I have avoided trying to spell out specific activities to accomplish the care and feeding of spiritual infants because I feel that a proper biblical *attitude* toward the babe in Christ must exist in order for the activities to have the desired effect in Christian growth.

The right activity with the wrong attitude can do more harm than good; the wrong activity with the right attitude may result in spiritual advance; but the optimum is the right activity with the right attitude.

In John 6:39 the Lord Jesus says, "And this is the Father's will which hath sent me, that of all which he hath given me I should lose nothing, but should raise it up again at the last day." Ultimately only Christ can keep what Christ has called and converted. But the instrument through which the Spirit of Christ may wish to work his keeping grace is you and me.

May our zeal for the will of God be such that we are willing to ditch old ideas and prejudices and see the initial grace of God in the babes for what it is, so that we may give ourselves utterly to the care and feeding of the infants that our Savior "should lose nothing."[4]

7

The Breakout

IN WORLD WAR II when the invading forces secured their beachhead and were dug in, they began receiving reinforcements in men and equipment. During this build-up period, the beachhead would be subjected to frequent counterattacks which would have to be repulsed. But even these attacks had their value. It gave our forces the opportunity to feel out the enemy and gauge both his strength and his ability. It also was a time to discover his weak points, to probe with patrols and plan for that moment when a major assault against the enemy lines could be launched.

Because these friendly forces were compressed into a small area, it left them particularly vulnerable. Therefore, the bigger the build-up the more pressing the need to carry the attack to the enemy and break out of the confining perimeters of the beachhead. More maneuvering room was needed, and that could only come by capturing more real estate from the enemy.

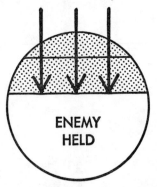

ENEMY
HELD

So also the situation for the "beachhead baby" Christian. In the last chapter we discussed the patient "build-up" process which lands the reinforcements of God in the beachhead area

of the new believer's life. There then comes
that crucial moment when the forces of God have to
break out of the original perimeters and capture
new territory in the life.

When a new believer has the input of the Word of
God, fellowship in prayer, and fellowship with
other Christian believers, it is inevitable that
the new wine of God's new life in him is going to
pressure a breakout. It may take time to build
up that pressure, but it will come. This is why
the Lord Jesus Christ likened the infusion
of his Holy Spirit into the believer's life to the
fermentation process that takes place in new wine.
He says, "And who would use old wineskins
to store new wine? For the old skins would burst
with the pressure, and the wine would be
spilled and the skins ruined. Only new wineskins
are used to store new wine. That way both are
preserved."[1] As new and flexible wineskins allowed
the expansion of the wine, so also the perimeters
of the believer's beachhead must be flexed and
ready to bulge out and encompass new territory as
the Spirit of God breaks out for growth.

Tragically, many Christians spend most of their
lives in a build-up process and never break out.
One can only marvel at how they can stand
the internal pressure that must be precipitated by
their attendance at church, listening to the
Word of God preached, plus what it must do to
them to see other Christians breaking out of their
perimeters and experiencing the new joy of
bringing new areas of their lives under the domination of the Holy Spirit. It is appalling that so
often the church has become the guardian of the
status quo, all the while preaching a gospel
of never ending change. What an irony this is!
But, perhaps it reflects the condition of members

lifted to a corporate level of stalemate.
Leighton Ford once said of the church, "It
would seem that the church only prepares to
move out after it has been run over from
behind!"[2] He was speaking of the church's
reluctance to take a forward stance and move out
in expressing itself on grinding social issues.
But perhaps the same illustration applies to the individual who has Christ in a beachhead in his
life, and only tends to move out when he, too, has
been run over from behind by shattering
circumstances that demand that he break out into
new patterns of growth.

   I don't know of anything that makes me
cringe on the inside more than for somebody to clap
me on the shoulder, and say, "Good old Lane,
you never change!" It wouldn't be so bad if
comments like that were made about a person's
reliability, steadfastness, and reactions of
pure love, but in my case, it seems that each time
it has been said it was in response to some
reaction that I had evidenced that, indeed,
indicated a certain rigidity in me that made the
statement truer than I would like to admit.
For the Christian, change is the name of the game.
Not capricious or whimsical change, but purposeful,
steady change that is moving us toward
the specific goal that God has in mind for our
lives. This is what Paul was talking about when
he said, "So, whatever it takes, I will be
one who lives in the fresh newness of life of those
who are alive from the dead. I don't mean to
say I'm perfect. I haven't learned all I should even
yet, but I keep working toward that day
when I will finally be all that Christ saved me
for and wants me to be. No, dear brothers, I am
still not all I should be but I am bringing

all of my energies to bear on this one thing: forgetting
the past and looking forward to what lies ahead,
I strain to reach the end of the race and receive
the prize for which God is calling us up to
heaven because of what Christ Jesus did for us."[3]

And one thing we can all be certain of, that
is, that this pattern of God breaking out of the
perimeters that we have set for him is intended
by him to go on endlessly in our lives. At
least, that's the way it's been for me in the
quarter-century-plus that I've known Christ.
About the time I feel that I can really be
at ease in Zion I sense that God is readying
another build-up in order to launch another attack
on the enemy in me, and take new territory
that I have either had obscured from my
view deep in my unconscious mind, or have in
plain view and just out of pure stubbornness have
restrained God from getting into.

In World War II the genius of the Japanese
for concealment was amazing. They could dig into
caves and find places to hide that at times
seemed almost impervious to whatever we could
throw at them in order to root them out.

So also I believe that one of the tragic
misunderstandings of today's Christian world is how
basically corrupt our old evil nature really is.
I don't think that Jeremiah was kidding
when he said, "The heart is deceitful above
all things and utterly corrupt; who can know it?"[4]
One of the reasons why we have misunderstood
how long it takes to bring about maturity
is that we have *said* we believed statements like
the one from Jeremiah, but in actual fact we have
acted as though our corruption was of easy
and quick solution.

Jesus also echoed Jeremiah's estimate of the

condition of the human heart when he said, "What comes out of the man defiles him; for from within, out of a man's heart, wicked reasonings proceed, unchastities, thefts, murders, adulteries, covetings, wickedness, falsehood, lewdness, an evil eye, blasphemy, pride, thoughtlessness. All these wicked things come from the inside and defile the person."[5] If we

really faced the depth of corruption that exists in that unconquered part of our islands and admitted the same, I don't think that we would be quite so surprised over the bickerings and divisions, criticisms and downright hostilities that are often evident between sincerely redeemed people inside the church. Perhaps my problem is the problem that everyone else has: I'm perfectly delighted to recognize all of this corruption in everyone else but hard put to it to face it within myself. It is only when I do face this condition in me and welcome the build-up of God's forces that I am prepared to cooperate and even hasten the breakouts in my life that God wants to accomplish. Most of us want God to do more about the evil in the world, but few of us really want God to start working on the world's evil by working on the evil in us.

So, regardless of where we are in our Christian life, whether beachhead babies, or people whose island is half occupied by the forces of God, we can rest assured that God wants to break out of the perimeters we have established for him. As in war, there will be death and bloodshed to accomplish this objective. I've come to believe that this is what Paul meant when he said, "I die daily." The advance of the life of God is dependent upon the death of another part of self. Why I resist God's

breakouts to such an extent is a puzzle to me.
Especially when I remember that in spite
of the pain of dying to self, there is such great
joy and comfort in having a new area of
my life occupied by the Spirit who brings love and
joy and peace to that area.

A comedian friend of mine used to tell
the story of a man who took Carters Little Liver
Pills all his life. He said that when that
fellow died, they had to take a big stick and beat
his liver to death. I really identify with that
classic illustration of the enemy-held part of me. That
part of me is worse than a cat for having nine
lives. Instead of taking a big stick to beat it
to death, I take the sword of the Spirit,
which is the Word of God, and give it a good
going over every day.

"Onward Christian Soldiers" would be a good
hymn to sing at the beginning of every day, but only
if we realized that the war that we're marching to
is far more internal than it is external.

8

Whose Side Are You On?

I HAVE NO IDEA where this story started. It's too good an illustration not to use simply because you don't know the source. A Black preacher was once asked what it felt like on the inside to be a Christian. He silently mused on the subject for a bit and then said, "Well, it's sort of like I've got two dogs inside of me. One is a good dog and the other is a bad dog, and they's always fightin'!"

His questioner, wanting more information, said, "Which dog is winning the fight?"

"Whichever one Ah says, 'sic 'em' to!"

Isn't that description a beaut? A punch line on that story that is equally profound—when asked which dog is winning, the answer is, "Whichever one Ah feeds!" Either way the story is told it presents us with a very basic question that has to be answered not only once, but almost on a daily basis.

The question is, *Whose side are you on* in this private war that you've got going on inside yourself? You might say, well, doesn't a person decide when he invites Jesus Christ to invade his own personal island that he is on God's side, and that's settled? Well, theoretically, I suppose, it is settled, but in actual practice I find that I have to re-settle that issue day after day. For instance, every day I have to decide whether I'm going to feed the new nature on the Word of God and prayer and fellowship with likeminded believers, or whether I'm going to do those things that will actually co-operate with the worse side of me. I find I'm great for theory in broad sweeping generalizations, but often hard put to it to work that theory out in practical daily experience in which I'm actually obedient to the commands of God.

One such command would be Jesus' statement, "But seek ye *first* the Kingdom of God and his righteousness, and all these things shall be added unto you."[1] Just today, for instance, after an exhausting schedule last night, I couldn't manage to struggle out of bed at the hour my clock went off, and it set everything running late so that my time of devotions got squeezed out. Like a jerk I sacrificed the best for something that was really quite good. I wanted to get on with writing this book, but didn't really give enough time to feeding the new nature and saying "sic 'em" to the Holy Spirit at work in my island.

Yes, I'm still having this struggle on a daily basis, even after knowing Christ over a quarter of a century. I would gather that Paul wrote the book of Galatians about the time when he had known Christ somewhere between twenty and thirty years, so I'll simply cite what he said. "I advise you to obey only the Holy Spirit's instructions. He will tell you where to go and what to do, and then you won't always be doing the wrong things your evil nature wants you to. For we naturally love to do evil things that are just the opposite from the things that the Holy Spirit tells us to do; and the good things we want to do when the Spirit has his way with us are just the opposite of our natural desires. These two forces within us are constantly fighting each other to win control over us and our wishes are never free from their pressures."[2] It would seem from this that Paul was making daily decisions concerning whether or not to obey the Holy Spirit's instructions, or whether to follow his natural (and I might add, normal) inclinations to pursue what his old enemy-held nature wanted him to do.

As a matter of fact, he goes on to indicate what happens when you don't obey the Holy Spirit's instructions. He says, "But when you follow your own wrong inclinations your lives will produce these evil results: impure thoughts, eagerness for lustful pleasure, idolatry, spiritism (that is, encouraging the activity of demons), hatred and fighting, jealousy and anger, constant effort to get the best for yourself, complaints and criticisms, the feeling that everyone else is wrong except those in your own little group—and there

will be wrong doctrine, envy, murder, drunkenness, wild parties, and all that sort of thing. Let me tell you again as I have before, that anyone living that sort of life will not inherit the Kingdom of God."[3] It might be well to ask ourselves a question, "How did Paul know that following your own natural, evil inclinations would produce that kind of result?" The answer probably is that some of that he observed in others, but a great deal of it he observed in himself. So, there is really a basic decision that we need to come to: *Whose side are you on?* Paul put it this way, "Don't you realize that you can choose your own master? You can choose sin (with death) or else obedience (with acquittal). The one to whom you offer yourself—he will take you and be your master and you will be his slave."[4]

There is a sense in which we do make an initial decision to make Jesus Christ and his Spirit our Master by declaring that we intend to obey him. But there is also a sense in which if we are going to make periodic breakouts and advances in this internal war, that we are going to have to cooperate with God by participating and allowing him to have a daily buildup within us to prepare for that next breakout in which he takes new territory. Since almost no one has really faced how long it takes to move from being a beachhead baby to being a well occupied island or, in other words, to go from spiritual infancy to spiritual maturity, well-meaning but misguided Christians have consistently implied that one can have instant maturity. I'm well aware of the fact that if pressed on such a contention, people would deny that that's really what they're saying. But whether explicitly or implicitly, that is actually what is often heard by the baby Christian. We live in a day when we can get instant coffee, instant iced tea, and even instant grits (thrown in for the benefit of any Southern readers). But I deny categorically the possibility of instant spiritual maturity. The danger is that people are offering what look like beautiful shortcuts to becoming a mature believer.

The first shortcut is the trap of legalism. Legalism is the notion that Christian maturity is demonstrated by certain negative behaviors. If you perform these negative behaviors by not doing this, or not drinking that, or by staying away from this place, or not engaging in that habit, then the idea is, you indicate that you have moved to spiritual maturity. Some churches even take these rules that are basically manmade and put them on signs prominently displayed in the church house. Christian institutions of higher learning oftentimes require students to sign a pledge concerning these negative behaviors. Whereas they do not come right out and indicate that performance of the pledge automatically makes you mature, it is at least there by implication.

Paul very directly spikes the incapacity of legalism to accomplish maturity when he says, "So don't let anyone criticize you for what you eat or drink, or for not celebrating Jewish holidays and feasts or new moon ceremonies or sabbaths. For these were only temporary rules

that ended when Christ came. They were
only shadows of the real thing—of Christ himself. . . .
Since you died, as it were, with Christ and this
has set you free from following the world's
ideas of how to be saved—by doing good and
obeying various rules—why do you keep right on
following them anyway, still bound by such
rules as not eating, tasting, or even touching certain
foods? Such rules are mere human teachings, for
food was made to be eaten and used up. These
rules may seem good, for rules of this kind
require strong devotion and are humiliating and hard
on the body, but they have no effect when it comes
to conquering a person's evil thoughts and desires.
They only make him proud."[5]

I was speaking at a conference one day on this
subject, and after I sat down my friend Fred Smith
got up and offered three penetrating reasons why
legalism would never do for bringing maturity. His
three reasons were: (1) a legalistic list of behaviors lets you know when you "arrive" and, therefore, produces pride. (2) Keeping a list of rules
lets you know who you are better than, and that
produces pride. (3) With the devious nature of the
human mind any list of legal rules was designed
to be "got around."

Just find a legalistic group of Christians and
I'll show you a bunch of people who are
usually looking down their noses at others who
are not following the rules that they have set up. The
funny thing about it is that this concept of maturity
is very geographical. All you have to do is
travel a few hundred miles and the list
of rules changes. If you go to a different country,
you oftentimes find radical differences in what
fits the list. Jesus said it, and it still stands,
"By this shall all men know that you are my

disciples in that you have love one to another."[6]

One of the grave dangers of a purely legalistic approach to the Christian life is that it tends to produce a vacuum in the life. When Christian maturity is equated with the removal of bad habits, instead of their replacement by the invading power of the Holy Spirit, the emptying process may in itself cave in a new Christian. The illustration of an empty glass is pertinent to this point. How do you get all of the air out of an empty glass? Anyone who knows anything about physics knows that there is no such thing as a perfect vacuum, and if you should try to get all the air out of a glass, the atmospheric pressure would make it collapse. So also, the life from which bad behavior habits are removed without an adequate replacement. One can get all the air out of a glass simply by filling it with water. The air is forced out of the glass by what's coming into it. Ideally, this is the way unbiblical behavior should be forced out of a life—but merely to make of the Christian life the negating of unbiblical behavior will produce a vacuum. The pressure of the world will often cave a young Christian in if he has been taught this way of instant maturity.

Another legalistic trap that has to be carefully spiked is the notion that a Christian education produces maturity. The theory seems to be that if you just cram enough Bible facts and theology into a person's skull, it is automatically going to produce maturity. It has surely been my observation that the mere acquisition of information does not automatically produce spiritual maturity. As a matter of fact, it can produce frustration of the most gigantic sort. The reason is not hard to find.

Oftentimes, when you have jammed tremendous
information about the requirements of the
Christian life into a person's head, it produces
frustration because he can think so far beyond where
he can perform. His theory is so much better than
his practice that he is overwhelmed with a
gigantic sense of guilt over his own hypocrisy. Simply
knowing something does not produce in the
knower the automatic capacity for doing.

Consequently, when a person acquires a gigantic
amount of information in a hurry, he may be
almost totally immobilized over his inability to
implement the demands of that information in his
own life. Certainly, I'm not against education.
I think it is a crucial aspect of Christian
nurture. But cram courses are often inflicted on
people readying themselves for church related
vocations. This puts them next to despair
because their lips can so far outdistance their lives.
If this were my isolated experience, I would
be ready to accuse myself of projecting
my needs to others. But in my contact with clergy all
over the English-speaking world I have come to
realize that many of them have experienced and are
experiencing precisely this frustration. Tragically,
never having been warned about such a possibility,
and having no one else talk openly about it,
they falsely assume that they, and they only, have
this problem. Jesus said, "If you know these
things, happy are you if you do them."[7]
It stands to reason then, if our knowing outruns
our doing that we are going to be grossly unhappy.

One night Annette and I were eating in a
restaurant, and just as we were finishing our
meal, two young men and a young lady came
over to our table and introduced themselves.
Their address and manner indicated that

they were people who had found Jesus Christ
right out of this modern street scene. The
one was carrying a Bible big enough to serve any
church as a pulpit Bible. They had heard me
speak somewhere and came over to have
a bit of fellowship. None of the three had been
Christians for very long, but all were quite
eager in their new life in Jesus Christ. Later, as we
were driving home, Annette said to me, "Those

kids are quite amazing, aren't they? They know so
little, but they are doing so much of what
they know, whereas we know so much and do so
little of the total that we know." Perhaps the
very reason for the radiance and happiness of those
kids was that they were proceeding at a rate of
doing that matched the acquisition of what
they were learning.

I'm aware of the fact that you can't do
something until you know it, and that therefore the
acquisition of knowledge has to be accomplished
prior to implementing that knowledge. What
I am suggesting is that we too frequently
oversell the effectiveness of acquiring a great deal of
knowledge in a hurry. I believe that our
education process should blend the sharing of
knowledge with the capacity to implement that
knowledge in the life.

Could this possibly be why the writer of
Ecclesiastes said, "I applied my heart to know
wisdom and knowledge, madness and folly. I
discovered that this, too, is chasing after
wind. *For in more wisdom is more vexation, and
increasing one's knowledge increases one's distress.*"[8]
Our beloved friend Pat Hunter once said,
"King Solomon wrote two thousand proverbs and
when the chips were down he couldn't find
the capacity to obey them." In other words, his

knowledge gave him the ability to see and
even to teach so much better than he could do.

It's interesting to note that only Jesus of
Nazareth, among all of the religious figures
of the world, was able to live up to the standard of
behavior which he taught. Perhaps one of the
things we should carefully rethink is the
pace we set in imparting knowledge to a new
Christian. Jesus alone could do what he knew.
Could it be then, that cramming people too full of
information may actually end up being a distress
if they have no ability to implement anything
more than a fraction of this knowledge?

The other trap that has so often been sincerely
offered to the new Christian, and to the
old, as a shortcut to maturity has been the "special
experience." This might range from a blurb in a
brochure announcing a special conference—
"Come to this conference and get it all together!"—to
those Christian groups that are advertising the
idea that a special experience of the Holy Spirit
is going to really get you over the hump and
on the right side of maturity. I do not deny in any
way the possibility of one being "filled with
the Spirit." What I do deny—and I think the
Bible supports me—is the idea that anyone is
ever totally filled with the Spirit to the extent that he
obliterates that enemy-held part of him which is
in his unconscious mind. To indicate such
implies a perfectionism that is not reflected in any
Christian life I have ever seen. It surely is not
reflected in mine, although I have "totally
surrendered" and "asked for the filling of the Spirit"
on innumerable occasions. What usually had
happened on such occasions was that the Holy
Spirit had revealed a new area of my life that needed
to come under his dominance. My new total

surrender was the giving up of territory that I did not know about until the Holy Spirit revealed it to me. I surely do not despise, disparage, nor in any way invalidate these experiences. I'm suggesting that what they add up to in the long run is simply the capture of more territory by the Holy Spirit. In other words, the Holy Spirit has broken out of the perimeters that we had established for him, and in this new experience he has taken new territory.

I was asked once to bring a message to the entire Christian education department of one of the most dynamic Pentecostal churches I have ever seen. They fully believed in the filling of the Holy Spirit, and as far as I know, they still do. However, when I drew the diagram of the enemy-held island and the invasion, the establishing of the beachhead and the concept of breakouts, there was general acknowledgement that this was precisely that which had been their experience. I spoke directly to the issue of being filled with the Holy Spirit and the experience of "speaking in tongues." I asked this question, "Isn't it true, that after you had spoken in tongues, experienced the fullness of the Holy Spirit, and had lived with this for a period of time, you discovered that the actual impact in your life had been somewhat oversold before you had experienced it? Isn't it true that what actually happened was that God got a new section of your enemy-held island, but he did not in any way take the whole thing at the time?"

The responding chorus of "Amen!" let me know that I had struck a deep responsive chord in their understanding of the nature of what had happened to them in this "special experience."

Paul speaks directly to this situation of the special experience in the same chapter in which he spiked the inefficiency of legalism. He says, "Don't let anyone declare you lost when you refuse to worship angels, as they say you must. They have seen a vision, they say, and *know you should.* These proud men have a very clever imagination. But they are not connected to Christ, the head to which all of us who are his body are joined; for we are joined together by his strong sinews and we grow only as we get our nourishment and strength from him."[9]

What I hear Paul saying here is that all of us tend to want everyone else to have the same kind of experience that we have had. In this regard we always tend to want everybody to be converted in the same way we have been, or else we tend to look with some skepticism on the reality of their conversion. It's interesting that he also teaches in this passage that both the legalism and the "special experience" people are made proud by this dogmatic stance which they take and apply to everyone else. Friend, there is no such thing as instant maturity. I know of no shortcuts whatsoever in the realm of spiritual growth. In the next chapter we'll talk about how long it takes to arrive at a reasonable level of maturity. But for now I want to address myself to one more deep problem that comes out of this business of demanding that someone else have the same kind of "special experience" that we have had.

Any experience of the grace of God necessarily thrusts us into the realm of feelings. I know of nothing more difficult to describe than "a feeling." Recently I led a class of new members in a prayer of commitment wherein they received

Jesus Christ as Savior and Lord and asked to be filled with the Holy Spirit. The following week a lady posed the question that she had really expected that more would happen as a consequence of receiving the Holy Spirit. When I pressed her for what she meant, it got down to the fact that she had thought that there would be some sort of overwhelming feeling attendant to that act of faith. When I asked her to describe the kind of feeling she anticipated, she hesitated, and then said, "Well, I expected to have some sort of an overwhelming good feeling." I then asked her, "What does a good feeling feel like?" Then she floundered and simply responded, "Well, it feels good!" I suggested this to her, "Don't you suppose that a member of the Mafia feels good when he has just killed his worst enemy?" She agreed that he probably would, and then I asked her to define the difference between his feeling good and the kind of "feeling good" that she thought ought to attend the act of faith that I had led her in. This helped her see how treacherous it was when we tried to define feelings.

If we must have a "proper religious feeling," then how would we know if we'd had the right kind of feeling when we admit that feelings vary so and that definition is so impossible to accomplish. I am not saying that the reception of Jesus Christ and the filling of the Holy Spirit does not have as a by-product the possibility of feelings. What I am saying is that the danger of the special experience is the tendency to put one's faith in one's feeling rather than in the never-changing Word of Christ. In my own experience I lived the life of a spiritual yo-yo in the early stages until I learned that faith is to believe what God had said in spite of what I might feel.

It was then that my spiritual life began to level out. A sinus headache didn't make me feel that God had abandoned me, because the Word of God still said the same thing—that he loved me, and that he would never leave me nor forsake me. Paul says, "For we walk by faith, not by sight."[10] When you remember that sight is a sense perception, I do not believe it is straining the verse at all to paraphrase it, "For we walk by faith and not by feeling." I thank God when good feelings attend me, but I believe God when I am devoid of feelings that might confirm the reality of the truth of Jesus Christ.

One day in 1969 I was walking down a New York street with my friend Jerome Hines, of the Metropolitan Opera company. "Jerry, how are you and the Lord getting on?" I asked him.

He smiled down at me from the three- or four-inch advantage of his six-foot-six height, and replied gently, "Lane, the longer I live, the more I think of Jesus and the less I think of me."

What an excellent antidote to the toxic effect of concentrating on ourselves and our feelings!

Perhaps the greatest treachery found in an undue reliance on feelings is revealed when you look ahead toward the end of life. As one grows older the strong tendency of the majority of us is to feel worse than we did when we were young, vibrant, and full of the vitality of youth. And, in the process of time, we feel so bad one day that we die. This means that the person who is relying on his feelings to confirm his belief would discover that at the time he needed that reassurance the most, it would be the farthest from him.

I think of the story told me recently by a friend concerning her grandmother. The dear old saint had lived to be ninety-nine years old, had suffered a

great deal, and was quite infirm and losing
strength rapidly. Toward the end she exclaimed,
"The music is beautiful! Please turn it up!" Then she
called out to a daughter who had died when she
was only fifteen years old. Then to her mother
and dad. Just as suddenly she seemed to be back in
the full reality of this life, and with a smile on her
face said, "Of course, you couldn't turn up
the music, because you couldn't hear it!" I'm quite
certain that the dear old lady felt pretty
awful at the moment that she had this gigantic
revelation of what lay just beyond the veil of this life.
As a matter of fact, in just a few moments after
that she had left this life and was in the next.
Her faith had sustained her in her hour of greatest
need, and the presence and power of Jesus Christ
had brought forth a magnificent reassuring experience
in spite of the fact that physically she felt wretched.

Add to this the glowing testimonies of so many
hundreds and thousands of people who have
suffered much in this life in a physical way and yet
have had gigantic expressions of faith in Jesus
Christ which was devoid of any physical feelings.

These are illustrations of what it is to walk by
faith. So, beware of the "feeling trap" that is
part and parcel of that oversold promise of a
"special experience" that is somehow going to get you
home free to the area of maturity. How sincerely
the promise is offered, yet the "special experience"
only gains more new (and sometimes very important) territory for the Holy Spirit.

Let me offer one other word about the
importance of putting feelings in their proper place.
We live in a time in history when people have
been tyrannized by their own feelings. Particularly is
this so in the younger generations. There
is a strong tendency to do only that which one

"feels" like doing. There is no question that how one "feels" is important, but the real issue is what has caused one to feel the way he does feel.

Some years ago in a meeting convened by Dr. Norman Vincent Peale, there was a group of us who had been brought together for the purpose of getting to know and trust each other. No organization was planned, nor ever came out of that meeting. Basically, we were there to share what we had learned about evangelism, and some of the outstanding figures in that field were present. In the course of the meeting a well-known practicing psychologist told of a trauma that he had been going through in his own life because, he said, "I have discovered that feelings follow behavior instead of the other way around. Since all of the education in my profession has insisted that behavior is a result of one's feelings, it has been a trauma to unlearn the one and embrace the other." I asked him to expand on this startling announcement, suggesting that if what he said was right, it would revolutionize what was being taught in this realm. Seminaries and colleges would have to alter their psychological doctrine to embrace such a radical notion. By the time he had offered his rationale to support this contention, I was fully convinced.

Out of my own life it makes sense. Misbehavior has always produced a feeling of guilt in me. Guilt makes me feel lousy. How about you? When-ever I resist the temptation to do wrong, and my behaviors are right according to God's Word, I inevitably feel good about it.

How often though in my own life I have been so tyrannized by my feelings that I was reduced to immobility. One of my favorite indoor sports

has always been to feel sorry for myself.
Yet, I discovered an easy way out of the deep
depression that afflicts me when I feel sorry for
myself. Jesus said, "Whatsoever that you would
that men should do to you, do you even
also unto them."[11] When I'm tyrannized by my
feelings and become immobilized by my self-pity, I can
sit down and make a list a yard long of good
things that I wish other people would do
for me. All I have to do is take number one on
my list and do it for someone else, and the
dark clouds of depression begin to dissipate
in the warm sunshine of one simple act of
obedience. Let me go as far as number two or three
on the list and I am almost hysterical with joy.
Feelings do follow behavior when the behavior is designed to make the life obedient to the
loving word of Jesus Christ. "If you know
these things, happy are you if you *do* them."[12]
When you know what he wants and you do it,
you discover that the good doctor was right
—feelings do follow behavior.

Then how do we maintain a regular, steady
advance on that enemy-held part of our island? By
realizing that we are in for a long pull, and that
it's going to be a battle against that lesser
self all the way. We've got to decide whose side
we're on and cheer the Holy Spirit on as he seeks to
search out new territory to reveal to us in order
that we can surrender it to him. We've got to feed
God's side of this struggle with the only food
that God has ever offered—his Word. It was Jesus who
said, "Man shall not live by bread alone, but by
every word that proceeds out of the mouth of
God."[13] We must build up the invading force of
God with the kind of ammunition that he can
use in this struggle. It's going to be a long war.

9

It's a Long, Long War

IT IS HARD TO IMAGINE anything more discouraging to a new Christian than to discover that he is still afflicted with patterns of temptation and sin that he had come to Christ in order to get rid of. It's one thing to make an occasional blunder, but it's quite another thing to fail again and again in the same pattern of behavior. This is the kind of failure that I knew and described in chapter 1. It can manifest itself at the point of anyone's weakness. Doubts begin to creep in about either the reality of one's conversion or the power of Jesus Christ to deliver on what he has promised.

The reason for this is that most of us have been oversold, or misunderstood what was going to happen to us when we receive Christ into our lives. Plugging along in the Christian life, we keep hoping and praying that something will come along and a magic, overnight, total transformation is going to take place. It was while I was in seminary, having known Christ for about four years, that I began to ask people this burning question in my soul. How come it's taking me so long to get better? I just never could get a satisfactory answer that seemed to help me with my understanding. Then one day years later, in my Bible reading I ran across two verses in 1 Timothy. Here Paul says, "Reliable is the message and deserving of wholehearted acceptance that Christ Jesus came into the world to save sinners, of whom I am foremost. But I found mercy, so that to me, foremost, Jesus Christ might display his *unlimited patience,* to be an *example* to *all* who shall put their trust in Him for life eternal."[1]

I have italicized the words that leaped

out from the pages of the Bible and gripped
me with a life-transforming understanding.
Here in verse 15 Paul is announcing that Jesus
Christ came into the world to save sinners.
His use of the word *save* indicates the security of the
position that he knew he occupied because of the
finished work of Christ. But the phrase
of whom I am foremost indicates that
he still saw that his condition needed gigantic
continuing work by the Holy Spirit.

It was verse 16 that really got to me. Paul was
stating that his life was an example, or as other
translations put it, a pattern. He was offering
his life as that example to be looked to in
order to gain understanding about how God deals
with the worst of us, as well as the best of us.
By the use of the word *all* he indicates that his life
example was to apply to every believer in
the future, not just some. I hasten to add that it
means then that his life was an example
for the simplest believer, as well as the most profound
theological professor, the weakest saint, as well
as the strongest. It means everybody, and I'm
grateful for that, because that includes me.
But the greatest relief came to me when I saw that
Paul was stating that his life was an example
of the *unlimited patience of God*. It was when I read
those exciting words that I realized that patience
demands the employment of time. As my
dear professor Dr. Manford George Gutzke used
to say, "To be longsuffering (patient) one
has to be long-bothered!" I had been agonizing
over why my Christian development was so
perilously slow, and now here was the invitation of
God to examine the life of Paul to see how
long it took him to get to a point of maturity.
    With great excitement I flipped my Bible to the two

places I knew to be either biographical or autobiographical concerning Paul's life. I turned to Acts, chapter 9, which relates the conversion experience of Paul, and then I turned to Galatians, chapter 1, which was an autobiographical testimony that I remembered employed some indication of how much time had passed by in his life.

I urge you to read all of Acts 9 through Acts 13:3. The passage in Galatians is 1:13 through 2:2. You can condense what you are going to find by comparing and collating these two sections about the passage of time. What we are looking for is the discovery of how long it took Paul to get to a point of maturity where he could bear big responsibility. The chapters in Acts go from his conversion to his ordination for missionary service. As you know, Paul was a terrible persecutor of Christians. He did it for God's sake, he thought. Not content with making havoc of the Church in Jerusalem and Judea, he got the authority to go to Damascus where some Christians had fled, in order to bring them back to Jerusalem and throw them in jail. The Bible clearly states that the Apostle Paul's zeal in persecuting Christians was so severe that he helped to incite the mob that stoned Stephen to death, holding their coats while others obviously actually did the deadly deed. It's hard to imagine anybody more anti-Christian than Saul of Tarsus.

On the way to Damascus he sees a great light, he hears a voice which he discovers is the voice of Jesus. Blinded by what he has seen and stunned by what he has experienced, he is led by the hand into the city of Damascus. A frightened layman, Ananias, is sent by God to lay his hands upon Paul and pray for him that he

might receive both the Holy Spirit and his
sight. Ananias' prayer is answered, and Paul
is fully converted to Jesus Christ. In his Galatians
reporting of the same event that Dr. Luke reports
about in Acts, he says, "I did not speedily communicate with flesh and blood, neither did I go
up to Jerusalem to those who were apostles
before I was, but I went away into Arabia and
came back to Damascus."[2] Immediately in verse 18,

"Then after three years I went up to Jerusalem
to get acquainted with Cephas [Peter] and
stayed in his company for fifteen days; but I
saw no other apostle except James, the
brother of the Lord. And what I am writing to
you, observe in the presence of God that I am not
falsifying."[3] Exactly what point in time during this
three-year period Paul went into the Jewish
synagogue and preached is not clear, but Acts
simply says, "After considerable time [this phrase
undoubtedly includes the three years that
Paul is talking about in Galatians 1] the Jews
conspired to destroy him, but Saul got wind of their
plot. Day and night they watched the gates to kill
him; but his disciples took hold of him and by
night let him down over the wall in a basket."[4]
The main thing to see is that either way you look at
the sequence of events in Damascus and Arabia,
it was three years before Paul went up to
Jerusalem for the first time. The passage in
Galatians confirms this. But after the Arabian
and Damascus three-year period he went up to
Jerusalem. Now, get a load of this! The relationship
between Damascus and Jerusalem was good in
those days. Trade routes were open, and Christians were on those trade routes. Jerusalem
undoubtedly had heard about Saul of
Tarsus, and what had happened to him on the

way to Damascus. In the three-year span there must have been a reasonable amount of communication that had arrived in Jerusalem to let them know something of the significant events surrounding Saul of Tarsus. *Yet,* when he arrived in Jerusalem after that three-year time of meditation in the desert and communication with believers in Damascus, the disciples in Jerusalem would have nothing whatsoever to do with him. Acts 9:26 says, "On reaching Jerusalem he made efforts to associate with the disciples, and they were all afraid of him; they did not believe he was a disciple."[5] Imagine now, if you will, this remarkable thing. Ask yourself this question: Why were they afraid of Saul when he arrived on the scene after they had heard the stories that had come down from Damascus? The only reasonable explanation that my mind conceives is that when they saw him there was something about his outward appearance and behavior that so put them off that everyone of them rejected the possibility of his really being a Christian. All except one of the disciples, Barnabas, rejected him. His name meant "Son of Encouragement." Mr. Great Heart himself—Ole Barney. Could it be that after three years of knowing Christ under the circumstances that he had known him, there was yet so little outward evidence that the disciples were afraid of him? To me that seems to be the only reasonable explanation.

But true to his name, Barnabas looked beyond the outward appearance and behavior, and believed that Paul's conversion was real. He had the courage to stand up for someone that everyone else has rejected. But this is what Barnabas did, and it was for this reason that the disciples admitted Paul into fellowship. From Paul's account

in Galatians it would seem to have been a highly
limited fellowship at that. Remember now,
that Paul's first preaching experience in Damascus
had not exactly brought revival. It had brought a
riot, and it was because of that that they had had to
let Paul over the wall in a basket in order to get
him safely away into the Arabian desert.

It is Paul himself who admits in Galatians that
on his first visit he stayed in Jerusalem
only fifteen days. However, for one reason or
another, he omits telling why his visit there was
cut so short. Luke tells us why in Acts 9:28-30.
Paul preached in the Greek-speaking synagogue in
Jerusalem, and brought forth the same violent
reaction from his hearers. They sought to
kill him. I don't know about you, but if my first
efforts at preaching had brought two such
responses as that, I would have been so discouraged
in my soul, I don't think I would ever have
preached again. However, such was not to be the
case in the life of Paul. The Bible indicates
that after only fifteen days in Jerusalem, when the
disciples there learned of the plot to kill
Paul, "They conducted him to Caesarea and sent
him off to Tarsus."[6] Paul's comment in Galatians is,
"Afterward I went into the regions of Syria
and of Cilicia; but I remained personally unknown
to the Christian churches of Judea. They
only got it from hearsay, 'Our erstwhile persecutor
now preaches the faith he once laid waste.' "[7]
To get to Tarsus one has to go through
both Syria and Cilicia. It's understandable that
Paul would not want to remember some of the
specific humiliations that he received in the
cause of Christ. But Luke, that careful
historian, in the verse directly after the one indicating
that they sent Paul home, uses these almost

insulting words; *"Then* indeed the church
enjoyed peace all over Judea, Galilee, and Samaria,
strengthened within and progressing in reverence
of the Lord. And through the encouragement
of the Holy Spirit there was increase in
numbers."[8] What seems to be implied is that when
the trouble maker went home a revival broke
out. I realize that one could push that too far, but
it is an interesting succession of events to

speculate on. In the period directly after that, there
is no mention of the Apostle Paul through
the remainder of Acts 9, 10, and only at the very
end of chapter 11—verse 25—is there another
mention of the Apostle Paul. In Paul's account in
Galatians he clearly indicates in chapter 2,
verse 1, that it was some fourteen years later that
he got back to Jerusalem again. He remained
in Tarsus for that entire time. We have
no way of knowing what kind of ministry he had
there from the way the narrative of his life
is picked up in Acts 11:25. It states that Barnabas,
now ministering in Antioch in Syria, makes a
trip to Tarsus to look for Saul, and on finding
him brings him back to Antioch where he companied
with them for an entire year. According to
Luke, the second visit to Jerusalem by Saul took
place when he and Barnabas went to take the
money which the Christians in Antioch had
collected in order to meet the famine-caused needs
of the Christians in Judea.[9] Saul is not mentioned by
name again until chapter 12, verse 25, when it
indicates that Barnabas and Saul returned from
Jerusalem when they had finished their ministry there
and brought along John, surnamed Mark. It was
after this that the Holy Spirit said, "Set me
apart Barnabas and Saul for the work to which I
have called them. Then, after fasting and prayer and

laying on of hands, they sent them away. So then, they were sent out by the Holy Spirit."[10]

According to this then, the gap between Paul's conversion and his separation to a specific heavy responsibility was in the neighborhood of eighteen years. Three years in Damascus and the Arabian Desert, fifteen days in Jerusalem on the first trip, fourteen years in Tarsus, and a year in Antioch during which time he made his second visit to Jerusalem. That adds up to eighteen years, or thereabouts, before the heavy responsibility of ordination was laid upon Paul.

I shrink inside when I think of the times I have mounted the pulpit, recited the conversion experience of the Apostle Paul, and then indicated that he went out and turned the world upside down for Jesus Christ *immediately*. This simply was not the case. There is difference of opinion among scholars concerning New Testament dating. But it seems rather plain that many years went by before the Holy Spirit laid the dramatic burden on Paul as a missionary of the cross.

I do not for one moment mean to imply that Paul was not busily engaged witnessing for Christ all the way through this period of time. However, at least in the early years his effectiveness as a communicator was somewhat less than a spectacular success, according to the Bible. Undoubtedly, it was out of his own personal experience that Paul said to the young pastor Timothy, "Lay hands of ordination on no one hastily."[11] Paul knew quite well that it had taken him years and years to reach a point of maturity that could bear responsibility. The blunders that the church has made in violating this biblical admonition are too numerous to catalogue.

What I'm pleading for is that all of us see

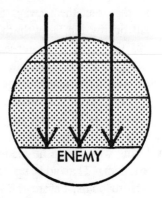

ENEMY

that it takes a long time to bring a spiritual infant
with a tiny beachhead to a point of reasonable
maturity. Paul's life is an example for all of the
unlimited patience of God. Let's rejoice in it, let's
bathe in it, let's comfort ourselves in it. Let's
be patient with one another as we're in
this process of growing. It's painful for all of us to
face ourselves and get in touch with painful data
and put it under the domination of the Holy
Spirit. I do not, for one minute, intend to
condone evil within us. God knows, and I know,
that I would like to be done with all of the
evil within me right now. But let's face it, that just
doesn't seem to be God's way. I remember
another memorable quote from my friend
Manford Gutzke as he was relating the zeal that
he knew as a new Christian. Then he enrolled
in a Bible college and took a course in Church
History. He said, "That's when I realized
that God didn't seem to be in much of a hurry. That
being the case, instead of rushing off to the
mission field I decided that there was time for me
to get a good sound education!" If ever
there was a place where the old axiom, "Haste makes
waste,"[12] is true, it's in the care and feeding of newborn Christians.

When I was a kid and growing my first row of vegetables or flowers, I had the philosophy that if a little fertilizer was good, a lot was better. Much to my dismay, I discovered that I had burned up my young plants. Fertilizer actually increases growth to the point where a plant literally burns itself out trying to use up all of the food it has been given. I honestly feel that we in the church have frequently been guilty of the very same thing. There is nothing which we need more than a sense of pace in bringing young Christians along. I think we need this sense of pace with ourselves, as well as with others. Somehow, we have got to make our approach to Christian education based more on one's spiritual age than on one's physical age. A thirty-five-year-old babe in Christ who is put into a Sunday school class that is considering predestination and election is probably going to get a little more fertilizer than he can use.

It's interesting that in our day we consider that a young man is old enough to go off and fight a war if he is eighteen years of age. I know that I was a lieutenant junior grade with all of my combat experience behind me before I was twenty-one years of age. I wonder if perhaps what Paul's life really tells us is that it takes just about as long to grow from a beachhead baby to reasonable spiritual maturity as it does to grow to a young man or a young woman. Could it not be that Paul had this in mind when he said, "But we were gentle among you as a mother feeding and caring for her own children. We loved you dearly—so dearly that we gave not only God's message but our own lives too."[13]

So many of us have been led to believe that maturity comes rather rapidly, that when it doesn't appear in us we become covered with guilt and quite certain that only we are plagued with the problem of slow spiritual development. As I have brought the essence of this message to various gatherings of ministers and Christian workers all over the world, it has warmed my heart to see the comfort that it has brought. I think of the young man in Melbourne, Australia, who came to me after hearing this message and broke down in tears. For just awhile, I held him in my arms, much as you would a baby. When he dried his eyes, he related the following story: He had been converted to Christ in a zealous, evangelical church. He had learned all the right things to say, all the right responses to give, and had excelled in verbal expression and in observing the right "don'ts" of behavior. His minister urged him to go right into Bible school. This he did after knowing Christ for only a year. He was so outstanding in his academics at Bible school that they asked him to remain as an instructor. He was fully equipped and could make all of the right sounds and express all of the seemingly right attitudes. Yet, inside he was spiritually a frightened little boy. He realized how spiritually young he was in point of time. He also came to see how dreadfully unfair he had been to himself, in making severe judgments about his absence of inner maturity.

I'm not suggesting we wait eighteen years to ordain people to ministry, but rather that we learn to gauge maturity by Bible standards. We must allow enough time for individuals to mature before saddling them with heavy responsibilities.

When my daughter, Susie, first went to school I remember on one of my visits there seeing a little boy about six years old whose eyes were

brimming with tears and whose chin was
beginning to quiver. You could see he was
terrified. His father took one look at him and in a
very stern and severe tone said, "Be a man!" The
one thing a six-year-old boy can't be is a man.
No way. He's a six-year-old boy, and he has a right
to be frightened at the prospect of all the
strangeness of school. Yet, for centuries this is what
we have been shouting at our feeble little babes
in Christ. Worse yet, we teach them to shout
it at themselves. No wonder so many live under
constant burden of guilt and self-accusation. It
takes time, time, time, and Paul's life is an
outstanding example of this. How good, though,
that his life also exhibits the unlimited patience
of a loving heavenly Father.

At one point in World War II, my squadron had
ridden out from Pearl Harbor to Saipan on a
British aircraft carrier. When we arrived, our ship
was nowhere in sight, so we were dropped on
the beach to live in tents until our ship did show
up. The enemy had been driven back into the
hills, but we could still hear the thump of
artillery fire from our position on the beach.

As was often the case in situations like that,
our troops set up for the showing of movies
in spite of the fact that the enemy was so near at hand.
There were three positions for movies on the
beach.

One night at one of the showings, some rather
unusual high-pitched laughter was noticed by
a member of the shore patrol. Upon investigation
he discovered two enemy soldiers sitting there
loudly enjoying our Mickey Mouse movies. It
was evident that they had run out of food up
in the mountains, had slipped through our
lines, stolen food and—what else would you

do after dinner?—were taking in a show. Such audacity! The enemy watching our Mickey Mouse movies!

I'm embarrassed to say that spiritually speaking, the same experience has been mine more times than I like to admit. In areas I had long since dedicated to Jesus Christ, I have detected the enemy carefully observing some of my Mickey Mouse fantasies. When and if it happens to you, just know that you have lots of company, and do to your enemy what the shore patrol did to ours that night. They hauled them out of there—they didn't even let them finish watching the cartoon!

What comfort to know that I'm not the only one it has taken a long time to get better. I'm in good company—no less a man than the Apostle Paul. "So comfort and encourage each other with this news."[14]

Spiritual maturity does not come automatically with the mere passage of years any more than physical maturity does. Life is sustained and growth is accomplished by good health habits— daily intake of good food and exercise. The same pattern must be observed to sustain spiritual life and growth. The food is the Bible[15] and exercising in godliness is hard work.[16]

The heights by great men reached and kept
Were not attained by sudden flight,
But they, while their companions slept,
Were toiling upward in the night.[17]

10

Too Much Too Soon

IN THE MOVIE *Dr. Zhivago* there is a
scene that is both horrible and instructive.
It is a gorgeous summer day and the Communist
forces, who are involved in the overthrow
of the czar, have taken up a position just in the
edge of a thick forest. From the vantage point of
the deep shade and the heavy growth, they

are lined up on their horses looking out over a
sundrenched open meadow. As the camera moves out
across this meadow with its waving grass, one
can see in the shimmering distance a troop of
the czar's soldiers marching across the field in
perfect order. Their loose-fitting white uniforms are
in stark contrast to the nondescript clothing of
the revolutionaries.

As the czar's troops move closer and closer,
one of the revolutionaries lifts up his rifle and
begins to take aim. The commander of the
Communist forces indicates that he is not ready for
firing to commence. Closer and closer the troops
march, directly into the ambush that is set for
them. Finally, when the troops are well within range,
the commander slowly lifts his rifle and takes
aim, followed by all of the other soldiers, and firing
commences. The first barrage decimates the
ranks of the czar's force. The others let out a cry
and begin to run instead of dropping into the
protective cover of the tall grass. What follows is
almost as though the revolutionaries were
observing target practice on humans. None of the
czar's troops can outdistance the guns leveled at
them. When the last soldier is down, the
firing ceases.

Now, the Communist forces ride slowly out to
make certain that their handiwork is complete.
As they near the scene of the carnage, several of

them dismount. As they approach the first prostrate forms, a bewildering childlike cry is heard, "Mama! Oh, Mama! Mama!" Quickly the revolutionary leader rolls over the first form from which the cries are coming, and discovers there, not a soldier but a young boy of about nine or ten years of age. In rapid succession other forms are examined, and the oldest of these soldiers would not exceed eleven or twelve years of age. Only the leader of the troop was a full-grown man, and even the hardened Communists are revolted by the idea that he would have led these children into battle.

It is a scene of sickening horror, but I wonder if it is not possible that the church has been, over the years, guilty of the same thing. If, indeed, it does take years to arrive at a level of spiritual maturity able to bear responsibility, and I think it does, then is it not possible that we have been dressing up spiritual children in the uniform of the King of kings and sending them out against an adversary for whom they were no match? All one has to do is look at the list of ministers demitting the ministry and Christian workers going into secular jobs to begin to realize that it may well be true. Add to that the number of missionaries sent out who have been shattered under the pressure of too much too soon, and the picture we see is not one of which the church can be rightly proud. "Lay hands on no man suddenly."[1] This is a biblical warning that we have failed to heed, and the ineffectiveness of many churches can be traced directly to the haste with which men have been ordained, both as ministers and as lay leaders, such as elders, deacons, stewards or vestrymen. Any of us who have been in on the organization of brand new

churches have seen bewildered men elected to high
office with no training and little qualification
other than the fact that they were present. The
truth of the matter is that one's spiritual
condition is not nearly so important to the electing
group as one's secular position. If a man is a
leader in the community, it is automatically assumed
he will, therefore, be a good leader in the church.

There have been those occasions where
unregenerate men have been elected to the
highest office that the church proffers simply
because they were men of influence and
affluence in the community. The fact that they might
be spiritual infants didn't even enter into the
thinking of those who proposed their names and
assisted their election. 1 Timothy 3:10
suggests that church officers first prove themselves
before they are elected and ordained.

As tragic as all of this is, there is yet another
category of Christians for whom my heart bleeds
even more. That is, the simple babe in Christ
who is placed in a church context where, with no
regard to his spiritual age, he is compelled
to assume positions of responsibility long, long before
he is ready. My own early days in the church
saw many blunders, not the least of which
was teaching people to traffic in unfelt truth—
demanding expressions of the gospel in a verbal way
that could not possibly be matched in the inner
recesses of the heart. These people were too
new to the Christian faith. I thank God for those
persons who resisted successfully my effort
to clap a mold on them that demanded too much
too soon. I am ashamed of the attrition rate
that took place among those who simply could not
bear the pressure of performing beyond their
experience, and so drifted away from all contact with

me or the church. I grant you, it could be that
some of them were just not truly converted
to Christ, but there also would be a large segment
of them who were, but who could not bear to
participate in the hypocrisy that was being thrust
upon them. If only I could have seen then what I see
now. But lest I curl myself up in a big ball of
guilt, I have to remember that I was afflicted by
teaching that never really came to grips with the
importance of pace and patience in bringing
the Christian along slowly, but surely, to a point of
maturity. I suppose part of it could also be
blamed on the fact that I was too much involved
in my own spiritual babyhood to be able to do
much more than deal with the incessant
crises that seemed to be plaguing my own existence.

When we continue to put people beyond their
depth in the Christian life, the strain involved
robs that life of the essential joy that one should
know in following Jesus Christ. Among the most
tragic developments of all has been the
tendency in the church to take those of us with
bizarre backgrounds and make us overnight sensations
on the evangelical testimony circuit. I don't
doubt the sincere motivation of those who vault
spiritual babies into national prominence
overnight. I'm sure they are quite proud of the
work of grace that God has wrought in a human
heart. But few of these people can handle this kind of
heavy publicity when they are so spiritually immature.

Donald Allen was a young man who had
everything going for him. Gifted with a plus
personality and rugged good looks, he was the idol of
his high school. Outstanding in athletics and
with the physique of a Greek god, he seemed to
have the world at his feet.

A devil-may-care attitude, however, combined

with a constant urge to demonstrate his manliness proved his undoing. Three times expelled from high school for drunkenness and unruly conduct he had finally hit the skids to a completely desolate life of debauchery. Arrested several times, he became the talk of the small town in which he lived. Neighborhood wags would shake their heads over him and whisper the latest gossip concerning his escapades.

It was at this low point in his life when he hit the skids that God stepped into his life. Converted during a special evangelistic campaign in a local church, his climb out of the gutter was even more startling than his descent had been. Invited to give his testimony the Sunday following his conversion he proved to be an effective public speaker. Seven accepted Christ as a result of his testimony. Invited to other churches to give his testimony to the grace of God he soon found himself in great demand as a speaker. Within two months he was holding his first evangelistic campaign with many more churches and religious organizations demanding his time. He seemed to be skyrocketing to the very pinnacle of Christian service.

A whirlwind courtship with a wonderful and gifted Christian musician seemed only to enhance his value as an evangelist. His wife played the marimba with exceptional ability. Together they seemed an ideal team. Then criticism began to come his way. This, combined with the fact he was not mature enough for the responsibilities of marriage, had a decidedly unsettling effect upon him. He became more and more remorseful and withdrawn in himself, often sitting in his room for hours and refusing to speak to anyone, even his wife.

Donald having no foundation under his crisis

conversion, seemed unable to understand that
the Christian life was intended to be a slow
but steady growth in the grace and knowledge of the
Lord Jesus Christ. The very fact that it had
proved to be no bed of roses seemed to leave him
bewildered. Still serving the Lord today as a
pastor, his whole Christian life has been one of abrupt
change and departure whenever criticism came his
way—often leaving a church without a
moment's notice. He regrets greatly today the
fact that he was shoved into Christian service so
fast after his conversion. His usefulness for the
cause of Christ has been greatly diminished because
he lacked the spiritual maturity necessary for
the demands made upon his time and talent.

   It would appear that the worse a person has
been in his pre-Christian days the more likely it is that
he will be made into an overnight celebrity
because misguided Christians expect too much
too soon. When the overnight Christian
hero finally falls on his face, these very ones who
encouraged him into getting his mouth so
far out in front of his life will be the first to have
nothing to do with him. With clucking tongue and
under-the-breath condemnation this dear
collapsed brother will be condemned for the
dishonor he has brought on the gospel. Granted that
every individual is responsible for the person
he becomes, there is yet gigantic responsibility
that must be borne by those who send spiritual infants to do the work of the mature.
   Such was the case of Brett Carson with a
checkered past in prison and self-wrought disaster.
His conversion made him an overnight
sensation in his particular denomination. Encouraged by the leaders around him and because of
the natural glibness of his tongue he was soon set

up with his own evangelistic team and tent, traveling from pillar to post and startling people with the diversity of his preaching. To me he said, "The day that I walked outside my tent to admire my six huge, shiny trucks and two magnificent Cadillacs was the beginning of my downward plunge. I became so insecure in myself that at the beginning of many crusades I would go to the men's room in order to overhear the ego-inflating comments being passed there about me. This was a necessary part of getting sufficiently psyched up, and the reassurance I needed to get through the night!"

Needless to say, the downward plunge that began when this young man viewed all the magnificent acquisitions of his spiritual success, ended at the bottom. However, the wealth he now had made it possible for him to set himself up in a lucrative business that allowed him to continue his life in a movie star manner. As these words are being penned he is just now, at thirty-five years of age, beginning a contact with me, honestly searching for a way back to a normal relationship with the Lord that he loves.

Why does this happen? I believe it happens because few of us have yet to understand what to expect as a result of Christian conversion. I believe it happens because few of us understand how long it takes to move from spiritual infancy to that level of maturity that can bear responsibility.

For every spectacular conversion turned catastrophe that we know about there are thousands of ordinary people whose lives reflect the same kind of spiritual disaster. The cause is the same—a lack of understanding concerning what actually happens at conversion, and, more important, what yet has to happen.

There are so many more cases that could be cited. Like the one I know of personally: a vicious young gang member, converted to Christ and exposed on national television within a brief span of time after his conversion. As he was seen all over the nation, the invitations came flooding in from all over the evangelical world. There seems to be an insatiable appetite for the hearing and the rehearing of this kind of bizarre story. Encouraged by so many invitations, and overzealous Christians, he formed his own evangelistic association. Wherever he went, he did the very best that he knew how to do. However, slowly but surely, the invitations began to diminish. Finally he accepted an invitation to work with youth in a local church. It was only the kind and patient care given him by the pastor that sustained him through the sense of rejection that had developed because those who had helped to make him prominent no longer seemed to have a burning interest in him. After all, his story had been heard by too great an audience for a repeat, yet this seeming indifference and dis-affection hurt. Through the guidance of the patient pastor, he is now really finding his gifts in a secular job, and doing Christian work on the side.

But the church's appetite for the sensational has not only a questionable effect upon the individual whose story is being used up and cast aside, it also has a bewildering impact on the simple believer who doesn't have that kind of a sensa-tional testimony to offer.

Just how devastating an impact this has on the nonsensational believer was illustrated for me in the comment I heard a man make to a friend as we were leaving a meeting where a sensational testimony had just been offered. His

words made me shudder! What the man had said was
not offered in bitterness or complaint, but, rather,
with a tone akin to wishfulness. He said it
during the coffeebreak at a luxurious retreat
center. What he said was his way of reacting to a
testimony we'd all just heard. The person
testifying had been one of those weird
Christian phenomenons called "a boy preacher."

After ordination at a ridiculously young
age, this man had become an alcoholic, left his
wife and kids, tried to kill himself, ended up
in a mental institution, and there had
emerged into a fullblown trust in Jesus Christ.
Through the love of Jesus and his new life in the
Holy Spirit, he had been restored to sanity,
reconciled to wife and children, and had
found a new fulfilling vocation outside of the ministry. It was a stunning testimony concerning the
power of our Savior, and during the coffeebreak
everyone was buzzing about it.

Now, about those words that made
me shudder—the plaintive words of the man
who was listening to everyone else rave
about the "great testimony." What he said was,
"Sometimes I wish I had been bad enough
to make it on to some Christian program for
a testimony!"

Understand, I can shudder over those words
without in any way detracting from the
marvel of what Jesus our Lord had done
for the testifier. I shuddered because of the
startling truth revealed about us evangelicals
in those words. A sordid past is almost
required if one is to fit into the category of
"great testimonies." We lionize and make
celebrities of people who have been
lifted out of the gutter of sin to a new life

in Jesus. Understand me, please! I praise
God for the power of Jesus to accomplish this, but
I believe the time has come for us to soberly consider what we are doing to all believers by this
tendency to exalt a prurient past. The most obvious
impact is on the average believer like the man who
uttered those words. Never a spectacular sinner,
he observed that what Jesus had done for him
didn't seem important enough to other Christians
to have him share his new life in Christ.

How often I have heard people say to me,
"I don't have much of a testimony. You see, I was
raised in a Christian home, and have always
loved Jesus, studied my Bible, gone to church, and
tried to witness in my own way."

Let's face it! That's the most glorious kind
of testimony to have. Glorious, because the
life has not been sullied by the grosser sins, nor the
body wounded by satanic violations of it.
Yet, we evangelicals have almost made a virtue out
of sin by our celebratizing those of us who have
wallowed in it prior to our conversion. It makes
one wonder if perhaps there isn't some sort of
an insidious vicarious enjoyment which the Christian
experiences in hearing a recitation of all of
another person's previous sins.

Another true story illustrates my point. A
beautiful young model had been led to Christ
by my wife. After a very brief period of time
she dropped by my study and ran off a rather
stunning list of invitations that she had to give her
testimony. Her testimony included a well
publicized divorce with all manner of immoral
accusations hurled around in the proceedings that
made good reading copy. When I evidenced
something less than gigantic enthusiasm over this list
of appearances for her, she asked me why. I asked

her to answer a question for me. I said to her, "If you were just a plain Jane who was not a photographic model, do you think you would have received these invitations to speak?"

"No," she said slowly, "I guess if I were just plain Jane, they would not have invited me."

I then asked her another question, "Would plain Jane's experience of Jesus Christ be any less valid than yours?"

Again, she responded, "No, I'm sure it wouldn't be!"

Then I said, "Do you suppose that what they are secretly interested in is your past life more than your present life, because that's the only difference between you and a plain Jane who has found Jesus Christ?"

I could see that my words stunned her, and it took her awhile to answer, but then she said, "Why, why. . .that's just awful."

"Yes," I said, "but the worse part of it is that these people are not in any way aware of what they are doing, either to you or to the plain Jane's who sit in the audience and wonder why no one ever invites them to give a public witness."

One of the things totally overlooked in reference to the "sensational testimony" that bespeaks a sordid background is the on-going impact that the sordid background has on the believer. Let me illustrate. Any way you look at it, Jacob was a cunning character, a deceiver, and, in some ways, a coward. It was not until he struggled with the angel of God that his nature was so changed and he got the new name of Israel. But the Bible indicates that Jacob limped away from that encounter, and limped all the rest of his life.

My background would hardly fit under the category of sordidness that some have experienced, but it was bad enough for me to be glad that God has forgotten about it. I only wish I could. There is a real sense in which I have limped psychologically and emotionally because of those patterns of misbehavior that characterized my early life. Like Jacob, we have a new nature and a new name, but there is still enough of the old nature on hand to create a limp. There are scars. I know that I am forgiven in all eternity for these things. Yet, there are temporal consequences that I must live with the rest of my life.

Let me illustrate further. Here is an unmarried girl who is pregnant, and the young man who helped her get in that condition has shown his true colors by fleeing the scene. There is no way she can win in this situation. If she gets an abortion, her conscience is stuck with this for the rest of her life. If she has the baby and puts it out for adoption, she forever wonders where the baby is, who it's living with, whether it is being treated right, or if it is even healthy. Every time she sees a child of that age, she's struck with a memory. Moreover, if she keeps the child, she and the child are then saddled with the perpetual reminder of the illegitimacy. Say in the course of the unwanted pregnancy and in the utter loneliness of it all, she comes to the saving knowledge of Jesus Christ—she knows that her sins are forgiven. Yet, there is a real sense in which she lives with the temporal consequence forever, regardless of which course she takes. Frequently, in the Christian world in our facile evangelical excitement over bizzare backgrounds, we will not even allow this kind of person to verbalize or face up to their psychological and emotional scars in our dogmatic insistence that in Christ all things are new. In view of the fact that our enemy-held islands are never totally conquered by God's forces on this side of Glory, we continue to suffer at least part of the consequences of past misbehavior.

Even as I say this, I want to plead guilty to my own charge. I have become so used to this pattern of operation that I almost do it without thinking. When I do think about it, I don't do it. I suppose you can say I'm reduced now to pleading with my readers to prayerfully, carefully, consider the impact, either of expecting too much too soon of the babe in Christ, or of turning those with bizarre backgrounds into overnight celebrities. This makes them overnight Christian leaders who simply do not have the spiritual maturity to proceed for very long without causing gigantic disappointment to many who have been led to look up to them. We must avoid exploitation at all costs. The price paid by everyone is just too high.

11

Child Prodigies?

IN EVERY AREA of art and academic discipline, history has recorded a few child prodigies. Television shows have been built around some of them who had amassed a gigantic amount of information at a very early age. Others have had mathematical skills that were mind boggling to say the least, particularly to those of us who find it difficult to balance a checkbook. At no point did anyone suggest a revision of education and its curriculum in order to provide a challenge to the exceptional. Only in recent days have there been those classes where exceptionally talented children could proceed at a faster rate than the rank and file.

Yet, I do believe that a case could be made for the idea that the church has geared itself up in its educational processes for the spiritual child prodigy instead of the rank and file. The exception has been mistaken for the rule.

If you have plugged along with me this far, it is probably true that most of you have thought of some individual whose experience of Jesus Christ simply will not fit into the slow developing pattern of growth that has been outlined here. I'm sure that such people exist, although I do not now find it possible to recall to my mind anyone that would fit into the category of a spiritual child prodigy. There may be somebody that you know who fits into that sort of category. There have been people that I thought would fit, but when I got to know them better I discovered that they were having the same sort of slow-growing pains that I had. However, I do not deny the possibility that such people exist anymore than I deny the existence of the exceptional child prodigy in other realms of intellectual and artistic pursuit. As I look back in my ministry, I realize that a pattern developed for me. I tended to give far more time and attention to those people who started with a healthy beachhead and developed more rapidly than I did to those who may have started with a fragmentary beachhead and developed slowly. Not only that, I tended to judge the slow growers severely on the basis of those whose outward indication of growth was more rapid. Far be it from me to project my failures upon the whole Christian church, but I do believe I detect a trend in myself that is everywhere reflected in our attitude toward the rank and file Christian. We have based our whole doctrine of spiritual progress (sanctification) either on the child prodigy or upon those whose growth pattern was far more rapid than the average. I believe that one of the reasons why many pastors tend to become disillusioned about the long-range results of an evangelistic campaign is that they leveled a standard of judgment on the average new believer that should have been reserved for the occasional spiritual prodigy or his second cousin, the big beachhead more rapid growth believer.

In checking my dictionary[1] for a clear definition of the word *prodigy,* I was struck by the similarity of the root word for *prodigy* and the root word for *prodigal.* The word *prodigy* comes from a Latin noun, *prodigium,* which means "omen, monster." What is indicated by the root word is that the exceptional child with remarkable and outstanding abilities is a little bit on the monstrous side when compared with the normal. The root word for *prodigal* comes from the Latin *prodigus,* or *prodigere,* which means "to drive away," or "squander." I was first struck with the dramatic similarity of the two Latin words, although one is listed as a noun and the other an adjective. Then I was struck with another idea, which

I would not want to press too far. That is,
I wonder how many people have been driving out
into a life of prodigality because of the unreal
standard of a prodigy which has been applied to
all. In the intellectual realm, if the standard of a
prodigy was applied to the average person, it
would drive him into utter despair over the possibility of ever attaining to that level of intellectual
proficency. Is it not possible that we have
been doing the same thing in the spiritual realm?
As I said, I would not want to press it too far,
but it is something that is striking, and should at
least be given serious thought.

In a sense, what I'm doing is admitting that
there may be exceptions to the rule that I am suggesting in connection with the spiritual development
of Paul's life based on an understanding of
Christian conversion being like the invasion of an
enemy-held island, and that the Christian
maturation process is like the invading forces'
strategy and warfare to take that island. I admit
to the possibility of an exception, but I am begging
us to contemplate the possibility that we may have
made the exception into the rule.

While I was pastoring a church at Key Biscayne,
I walked one day along the beach with Billy
Graham, who was visiting me. I was greatly
burdened by my lack of spiritual progress and I
poured out my concerns to my friend. To illustrate
my point, I took a stick and drew a line in
the sand. First I drew an intersecting line
to indicate the time of my conversion to Christ. Then,
close to that line, I indicated a point to represent
where I felt I was that day in my Christian life.

In contrast, I marked a spot in the sand, far
off to the right, representing the spiritual perfection
which I so much longed to attain.

"Billy, why am I making such slow progress
toward the place I feel God would have me be
in my Christian growth? Why does the maturing
take so long?"

Billy took the stick from my hand and marked
a spot behind the point I had used to indicate "where
I am today." "Lane," he said with characteristic
graciousness, "if you are *there,* I am only *here.*
The important thing to know is that the only hope
for either one of us is that the gap between our
achievement and the perfection of our Savior is covered by the blood of Christ."

Most of us are dreadfully embarrassed by
the total failure of the twelve disciples after some
three years of visible, physical companionship
with the Lord Jesus Christ. Let's face it,
their eyes had seen wonders that no human
eyes had even seen before. Their ears had heard
words like no other ears had ever heard, and their
lives had been touched with the love and compassion that had never existed before the time of Jesus. Yet, when the chips were down, they failed him.
One betrayed him, one denied him, and the rest
deserted. I grant you that they had not yet
received the Holy Spirit to give them the kind of
courage that would turn cowards into conquerors,
yet they had experienced Jesus Christ in the flesh
in ways that most of us envy. Anyway you look
at it, their development was slow. I remember one
of my seminary professors telling me that after
the resurrection of the Lord Jesus and the infilling
of the Holy Spirit on the day of Pentecost, God
finally had to resort to persecution in order to drive
the disciples out of Jerusalem so that they would
begin to fulfill his Great Commission. Although
I believe that God is sovereign, I would rather
attribute that persecution to the wickedness of men.

The delay in getting about the Great Commission
was part of God's plan. He was waiting for
them to mature to the point where they could
shoulder the responsibility.

Evangelicals traditionally have been somewhat embarrassed by a late dating of the New
Testament documents. Yet, if some of us love
John's Gospel the best, could it not be that it
was written from the vantage point of some sixty
years of experience with the living Christ
and with certain insights about the person and work
of Christ that only mature reflection could have
given him? When you see the love that exudes from
the pen of this "son of thunder," one can only assume a tremendous growth pattern from the time
that Jesus gave him that appropriate nickname.

Perhaps you know some child prodigies in the
Christian life. Wonderful! But let's not mistake
the exception for the rule. Most of us run-of-the-
mill Christians are slow growers. And the ground
which the invading Spirit of God gains in our
enemy-held island is a slow, tedious acquisition
for his invading forces. I kind of think that God
intended for us to enjoy the process. Yet, who could
possibly enjoy the process when an unreal standard
of development leaves him covered up with guilt
and self-accusation?

What blessed relief came to me the day I
realized for the first time that my lack of perfection was not a surprise to God at all. What overwhelming comfort came to me when I read these
words of the Apostle John, penned some sixty
years, at least, after the death and resurrection of our
Lord Jesus. He said, "If we say that we have no
sin, we are only fooling ourselves, and refusing
to accept the truth. But if we confess our sins
to him, he can be depended on to forgive us and

to cleanse us from every wrong. (And it is perfectly proper for God to do this for us because Christ died to wash away our sins.) If we claim we have not sinned, we are lying and calling God a liar, for he says we have sinned. My little children, I am telling you this so that you will stay away from sin. But if you sin, there is Someone to plead for you before the Father. His name is Jesus Christ, the one who is all that is good and who pleases God completely. He is the one who took God's wrath against our sins upon himself, and brought us into fellowship with God; and he is the forgiveness for our sins, and not only ours but all the world's."[2] As I read those words I stared in almost shocked unbelief at something I had never seen before. That was the collective, personal pronoun "we." John was including himself in the company of those who continued to need the forgiveness of the Lord Jesus Christ.

Out loud I spoke as though to the Apostle in person and said, "Oh, John! Are you telling me that after three years of companionship with the Savior in the flesh and sixty years of being filled with the Holy Spirit and companionship with the Savior in his invisible state, you were still 'blowing it' and needing the forgiveness of the Lord Jesus Christ? John, John, when you say, 'We have an advocate with the Father,' does that really mean that you continued to that very day and hour to need the advocacy of the one who is the sacrifice for our sins?" When the full implication of what I had read dawned on me, tears of relief filled my eyes.

It has been hard learning to be happy with the process. It's so humiliating to be tripped up again and again on the same stupid failings. Yet, I can thoroughly identify these days with the old Black preacher who said, "Ah knows Ah ain't what Ah ought to be! But Ah also knows Ah ain't what Ah used to be! And Ah thanks God Ah ain't what Ah'm goin' to be!" That's the only posture I know of that gives me the capacity to be happy in the process.

12

Paul Finally Had Them All, but It Took Time

THUS FAR everything that we have said
has pertained to the subject of the spiritual
maturing process. We have discussed the invasion
of a life by the Spirit of God and the internal Christian warfare necessary to bring maturity. The
goal toward which we are moving is summed up in
one word: *love*. What Jesus said is worth
repeating, "By this shall all men know that
you are my disciples, if you have love one toward
another."[1] This kind of love is going to reveal
itself in also producing a personality that is full
of "joy, peace, patience, kindness, goodness,
faithfulness, gentleness, and self-control."[2] That's
the fruit of the Spirit which Paul called, "A still more
excellent way."[3] The way that Paul spoke of is
well illustrated in his glorious chapter on love—1 Corinthians 13. This is the fruit of the Spirit. The
fruit of the Spirit should never be confused with
the gifts of the Spirit.

We live in a day when the mere mention of
the gifts of the Spirit arouses strong feelings
and potential controversy. The very controversy that
surrounds the whole idea of the gifts of the
Holy Spirit which God gives denies the fruit of
the Spirit in which those gifts must be exercised.
Our most profound beliefs must be held and expressed in love or we add up to nothing.[4]

In the New Testament there are four lists of the
gifts that the Holy Spirit brings: 1 Corinthians
12 and 14, Ephesians 4, Romans 12, and 1 Peter
4. Interestingly enough, each list of the gifts
differs from the others. None are identical.
The reason for the giving of these abilities by the
Holy Spirit is found in Hebrews 2:4, "God always
has shown us that these messages are true by
signs and wonders and various miracles and by

giving certain special abilities from the Holy Spirit to those who believe; yes, God has assigned such gifts to each of us."[5] The second thing to see is that the list of gifts is in reality God's worksheet for his people. This is what God expects us to do, and in order to accomplish his spiritual purposes in this world, he promises to give us the ability to do them.

It is my conviction that when the Holy Spirit enters the believer's life at conversion, he comes bringing the full potential of all his great gifts. Some will be made evident very early in the believer's experience—others may not become a reality until much later—some indeed may never be drawn upon, but all the potential is there, fully compatible with the believer's temperament and talents.

I have labored the point that the development of the fruit of the Spirit comes in a long, drawn-out dynamic process. Doesn't it just stand to reason that God would impart the gifts of the Holy Spirit to us in the same sort of long, drawn-out process? The absolutely marvelous thing about receiving the gifts in a developmental way is the fact that I'm never frozen in one position concerning the abilities that God gives to me. My future can always be brighter than my past. All one has to do is contrast the early life of Paul with the later life of Paul to see that he had not only developed the capacity to love, but had received additional abilities along the way that made him a far more proficient servant of Christ. I'm sure that people are sincere when they insist that everyone has received *a* gift, but I think we are shortchanging ourselves when we say that, as we shall shortly see. God has given me certain abilities now that I did not have ten years ago, and

I trust that he's going to give me certain abilities in the future that I do not have right now.

Unfortunately, the Bible itself is frequently used as an excuse for the exercise of one gift. Over and over again, with monotonous sameness, I have heard an exposition of Ephesians 4:11-13 that runs after this fashion. God has given to each man (usually in this case, they mean clergyman) a gift. The gifts that are listed in Ephesians 4 are, the gift of an apostle, the gift of a prophet, the gift of an evangelist, the gift of a pastor, and the gift of being a teacher. Since the Bible indicates that the person who has the gift of being an apostle must be someone who has seen the resurrected Christ, we will say that under ordinary circumstances that gift is no longer being conferred in our day. In my acquaintance there is only one man that I know of who has had a visible manifestation of the reigning Christ. This came in his conversion experience and has not been repeated since then. The aim of God in conferring these gifts on people in the church is that ". . . .we all may arrive at the unity of faith and that understanding of the Son of God that *brings completeness of personality,* tending toward the measure of the stature of the fullness of Christ."[6] The question I would like to pose is this: Can we say a person is complete if his only interest is evangelism? Can we say a person is complete if his only interest is pastoral care? Can we say a person is complete if his only interest is prophecy? Can we say a person has a complete personality if his only interest is teaching those who have already been won to Christ by someone else?

Consider this. The man who wrote these words was an apostle, he was a prophet, he was an evangelist, he was a pastor, and he was also a superb teacher. At various points in his life and ministry, he exercised one of these gifts in priority to the others, but not to the exclusion of them. In other words, by the time Paul wrote this letter to the Ephesians, he had all of the gifts that he mentioned in this list in Ephesians 4.

However, when we come to the present day institutional scene we find this list of gifts most frequently offered as an excuse to exercise a ministry and manifest a personality that is something far short of being complete.

I remember hearing Bishop Jack Dain, of Australia, tell of his growing years in the church in England. One of his vicars maintained that he had the gift of a teacher, and all he did was to utilize his pulpit opportunities for teaching that was over the heads of most of the people, but sounding fantastically profound all the while. After him came a vicar who maintained that he had the gift of evangelism. His ministry included only evangelistic sermons and calling people to faith in Christ. Lest I seem to be blaming these men, whom I do not know, may I hasten to say that they were probably victimized by the teaching which they had received concerning the singularity of gifts offered by the Holy Spirit. A man got one gift and he worked it to death much to the utter despair of the people to whom he was ministering.

Another tragic development in our whole understanding of the gifts is involved in the institutionalizing of the church. Let me show you what I mean. If I say the word "evangelist," who pops into your mind? Billy Graham, of course. If I say the word "teacher," there automatically looms before our individual minds some person within our Christian experience whose profound teaching was a blessing to us. If I say the word "pastor," then the man who comes to mind is the person who cared for us and visited us when we were sick and sought us out when we were missing from the regular gatherings of the flock. You see, we only associate these gifts with people who are into the institutional framework and who carry labels with them that inevitably mark them as clergy.

When we put ourselves in the context of the kind of church that existed when these words were penned, and the kind of people that God had gifted as leadership, it's hard to marry our present day institutional image with that one. What I'm saying is that these gifts were not exclusively set aside for the clergy, but were offered to one and all. Moreover, I'm maintaining that these gifts were not offered in exclusion of the other gifts.

If a man involves himself in a life given both to studying and uttering of prophecy and has no concern for the broader spiritual condition of the people that he addresses, then I think he is eccentric. The evangelist who has no pastoral concern for the babes in Christ that come under his ministry is eccentric and not complete. The pastor who only pastors, and the teacher who only teaches without an evangelistic concern for those persons who never have made a commitment to Christ is far from being a complete personality. We must not limit these gifts to the clergy, nor must we ever contemplate exercising these gifts apart from a conscious awareness of the necessity of exercising these other gifts. I spent nine years as an evangelist, and during that period of time had a genuine concern for the ministry that God gave me to my fellow ministers, as well as a concern for what happened to the babes in Christ after they had made their commitment. My concern extended to what kind of teaching they would receive, and whether they were aware of the potential of these days for the fulfillment of prophecy.

Perhaps the best illustration in my own life of the necessity of the multiple expression of these gifts came when I was conducting a Crusade in Christchurch, New Zealand. During the time of the Crusade when I preached to thousands of people, I had to exercise the gift of the evangelist. The ministers in the churches of Christchurch had invited me to conduct a city-wide campaign for the purpose of evangelism.

I then tried to sneak in a one-day vacation to Mt. Cook in the Southern Alps of New Zealand. In the seat behind me on the plane was a middle-aged American lady who constantly badgered me concerning what we were seeing out of the window. I knew little more than she did about the scenery outside, but, to satisfy her and amuse myself, I made up logical names for a lot of what I saw and offered them as explanations concerning the view. I deplaned at my appointed destination in the Alps, but she remained on the airplane.

When I arrived in my motel room, my phone was ringing. It was the director of the School of Evangelism being held in Auckland, New Zealand. The school was being offered in conjunction with the Billy Graham Crusade that had just begun in that city. It seems that I was to replace a couple of the fellows who could not teach in the School, and it necessitated my immediate return to the small airfield to try and catch the next flight back to Christchurch and connect on to Auckland. I was placed on standby, and I was the last person to board the plane, and who did I sit next to on the flight back to Christchurch? Right! The lady who had so intruded herself into my flight coming up to the Alps. This time I realized that my being next to her was no accident. Quietly I prayed that God would tell me what the situation was and make me sensitive to meet her needs.

As I began to question her about where she came from, and got her attention off of the scenery, I found her quite ready to talk. When she found out that I was a Christian, she really began to open up. It seems that she had been forced by financial necessity to put her aging mother in a nursing home. When she did this, the mother accused her of killing her. After about a year in the nursing home, the mother died. But her daughter was absolutely covered up with guilt, feeling that perhaps she *was* guilty of killing her mother by putting her into a nursing home. It did not matter that there was no other way to do it and still support mother, she still felt guilty. I also discovered that this woman was a person who believed that Jesus Christ was her Lord and Savior.

I then pulled out my Bible and opened it to 1 John 1:9. I had her read the words slowly out loud. "But if we confess our sins, he is faithful and just to forgive us our sins, and to cleanse us from all unrighteousness."[7] I had her read it two or three times, and then accused her of having made a mistake. I

said to her, "I think you made a mistake in
reading that. It doesn't say that God forgives
you for all of your sins. It says *some*, doesn't it?"
She apologized, and then started to read it again.
When she got to that little word *all*, she stopped and
said, "No, it doesn't say *some* sin, it says
all." It was then that she sucked her breath
in in a sound near to a sob. "Oh! Oh! It says
ALL!" I then assured her that she knew
and I knew that she had not killed her mother,
but that she had simply been victimized by
the circumstances. "However," I said, "let's
just imagine that somehow you were guilty.
Do you suppose that 'all' that we read about
would include that guilt?" Her eyes now
brimming with tears, she said softly, "Oh, yes, yes,
yes!" I then took her to many other verses
in the Bible speaking of the complete forgiveness
of our Lord Jesus Christ.

When we deplaned in Christchurch, she took
one of my hands in both of hers, and said, "I
believe God put you on that plane to meet my need.
Thank you. Oh, thank you!"

I then rushed to catch the next flight to
Auckland, dashed out of the airport, leaped
into a cab, rushed to the scene of the School of
Evangelism, almost immediately moved into the
pulpit, opened the Bible, and began to
teach the students there what I've been trying
to share with you here. That is, that Paul,
by the time he wrote what we have in the New
Testament, was an evidence of a multiplicity
of the gifts that he said the Holy Spirit would bring.

Retrace my steps with me. In Christchurch
the *need* before me elicited the gift of evangelism
within me. On the airplane returning from the
Southern Alps, the need beside me drew out the

gift of the pastor within me. When I stood before ministers and seminarians in Auckland, the need before me elicited the gift of the teacher within me. Paul had all of the gifts of the Holy Spirit mentioned in Ephesians 4. In case you are reading along and muttering to yourself, "But he was the Apostle Paul, and I'm just plain me!" Then I hasten to say that it was Paul himself who said, "But I found mercy, so that to me, foremost, Jesus Christ might display his *unlimited patience,* to be an *example* to *all* who shall put their trust in him for life eternal."[8] Friend, if after many years of growth in the fruit of the Spirit, Paul had also grown to exercise most, if not all of the gifts of the Holy Spirit, then why should we continue to be incomplete personalities? Should we not aspire patiently to develop to "That understanding of the Son of God that brings completeness of personality, tending toward the measure of the stature of the fullness of Christ"?[9]

It might be well to face up to whether or not we really want a multiplicity of the gifts of the Holy Spirit. The reason is easy to see. If we receive these gifts, then we automatically have a responsibility to develop that kind of radar-like sensitivity to pick up the needs of people that God puts in our way, and then let that need draw from us the specific gift that is going to meet their need. It's a stretching experience, and certainly does increase one's work load. Needs that you could walk right by with indifference before begin to grab at your heart. By faith you try to meet that need.

We live in a day of "specialists," and this day has afflicted the church no less than any other discipline. There are medical men who are so highly specialized that they would think it an insult to be asked to treat a symptom that lies only six inches away from their specialty. Lest we rush to condemn the doctors, we Christians have become just as bad.

Obviously, it took Paul a long while to develop this "completeness of personality" that he writes about. It takes refined, Holy Spirit sensitivity to respond to the real needs that people often camouflage. All too often we Christians spray our gifts on people without being sensitive to the need that the person really has. Let's don't be God's mouth to a person who at that time needs you to be God's ear. Don't be God's laugh to a person who at that moment needs you to be God's tear. The fruit of the Spirit represents the basic heart attitudes in which the gifts must be exercised. Otherwise, the best gifts become sounding brass and clanging cymbal.

One of the dangers in both physical life and spiritual life is that we often have an ability before we have the maturity to properly use it. For instance, humans are capable of having babies before they are mature enough to take care of them. They have the ability to procreate but not the maturity to offer the proper parental care. This frequently seems to be the case in the spiritual realm as well. We somehow receive the ability to share our faith in Jesus Christ before we have developed the maturity to really care for the spiritual baby that our gift may bring.

A friend of mine said the other day, "Isn't it nice that God arranged it so that a woman could not have a baby more frequently than every nine months?" What he was hinting at was the possibility that there might be very great advantage in Christians not being able to have more spiritual children than they had the time to take care of. I've often wondered what would happen if we evangelists really assumed the responsibility of the care and feeding of every spiritual baby we brought into the world. It would be my opinion that Billy Graham has probably done more to try to accomplish this through well-trained counselors and alert churches than any other evangelist in history. Yet, one of the frustrations that all of us had in those days when I was on the Graham Team was the lackadaisical attitude of the average church member toward really becoming a guardian angel to the people they had counseled in the Crusade.

Since we have already established Paul's life as an example to all of us who have come to believe in Christ, maybe we should look at his sensitivity and concern for his infant believers. This is what he said to a group of them, "But we were as gentle among you as a mother feeding and caring for her own children. We loved you dearly—so dearly that we gave you not only God's message, but our own lives too."[10] He was not only a prophet, he was an evangelist. He was not only an evangelist, he was a pastor. He was not only a pastor, he was also a teacher. It took time—a long time—but finally Paul had them all. Remember, too, that the Savior that Paul served also represented every one of those gifts as well. Since we are to be "conformed to the image of God's Son,"[11] perhaps the goal for which we should strive is the same one that brought Paul completeness of personality.

13

The Hardest Place to Win the Battle— at Home!

"I WILL TRY to walk a blameless path, but how I need your help, especially in my own home, where I long to act as I should."[1] I identify with those honest and straightforward words of the Psalmist.

A number of years ago there was a popular song whose words reflected the negative side of what the Psalmist said. It went like this: "You always hurt the one you love, the one you shouldn't hurt at all. You always take the sweetest rose and crush until the petals fall." It is a sad irony that this is so frequently true. Out of ego needs, we put our best foot forward for the people we care the least about, and our worst foot forward for the people who mean the most to us. The old Pennsylvania Dutch saying, "Vee iss too soon oldt, and too late schmartt!" certainly applies to this writer. It has taken me a long time to catch on to what I was doing to my family, and even longer to catch on to the reason for it.

I honestly believe that the hardest place in the world to live out your faith in a mature way is in your home. It is relatively easy to fake out the people on the outside, and give the distinct impression that you are an utterly mature person. It is at the core of your life, in your home, where the presence or absence of genuine Christian love makes itself known. I am impressed that much that I have learned over the years has been learned the hard way, and at great personal sacrifice on the part of those nearest and dearest to me. I'm sharing these hard gained insights about relationship in the home because I sincerely believe that this is where the measure of maturity must finally be taken.

The invading force of God in our enemy-held islands has got to make his presence known in this part of our lives, or we are just deluding ourselves. Many a minister's wife suffers in agonized silence over the hypocritical gap between her husband's "pulpit-posture-of-perfection" and the childish, ego-ridden man she has to live with at home. The same can be said for the wife and children of many lay leaders in the church as well. After the Sunday show at the church, the halo begins to slip askew, and if the leader is thwarted by the mate, the halo breaks in two and becomes horns. In my own case, I compounded that horror by suggesting that anyone who thwarted the great "man of God" at any point was surely an emissary from the devil himself. Surely not everyone is as dense or dull of hearing as I was, but the frequency with which one discovers unhappiness in Christian homes is indicative of the need to return to the Bible and take a second look at what it is suggesting as the basis for a Christian marriage.

I see the number one problem in the average home as being that of communication. In my case, I wanted to communicate, but my understanding of communication was merely to announce both my opinions and my desires with the thought that everything must then bend itself to please me. One thing I do know by now, and that is that communication has to be a two-way street in which each party really hears the other. There is no problem which is incapable of solution if two people are able to communicate without getting angry or hurt in the process. It doesn't matter whether it's a problem about raising the children, how to spend the money, sex, or where to spend a vacation. However, if two people are not able to communicate at a deep feeling level, then their efforts to solve problems usually end up creating more problems.

The causes for an incapacity to communicate with and understand each other are numerous. However, to my way of thinking, one of the most overlooked factors in regard to this whole problem is further complicated because we have bought into a premise that is untrue. That premise is presently being greatly complicated by certain aspects of the women's liberation movement. (I hasten to add that there are phases of the women's liberation movement that are long overdue for the education of us men and women.) This false premise is that men and women are the same, with minor differences found only in physical equipment. I believe that the Bible teaches that men and women are emotionally, psychologically, intellectually, volitionally, and constitutionally different from one another. I believe we are different in almost every conceivable way. My reason for saying this comes from the very creative act of God found in the book of Genesis. "And the Lord God said, 'It is not good that the man should be alone; therefore, I will make him a helper completing him.' "[2] In my understanding, you don't complete something by duplicating what is already there, but by adding what is missing. In other words, woman was created to be different from man by design. However, if we do not admit to the difference and yet find our mate responding and reacting in ways different from ourselves, then that difference becomes a threat. I believe that God meant the difference to be an adventure, not a threat.

The woman, then, is what is missing in the man,

and the man is what is missing in the woman. Somehow, though, we all get married expecting that
our mates will tend to respond to any given
set of circumstances in the same way we do. When
they don't, it comes as quite a shock and surprise. "I just don't see how you can look at it that
way!" This is the rejoinder frequently made by an
astonished mate. Given a succession of these
"strange" reactions to a series of situations, you have
each party beginning to be persuaded that he or
she married a very strange person. No, each
just married a member of the opposite sex.

Dr. Paul Popenoe[3] says that the unexpected
reaction from a member of the opposite sex probably
is the cause of more distress in marriage than any
other single thing that he has discovered in his
lifelong ministry to troubled marriages. You see,
nobody has warned any of us concerning how
different men and women really are. When we run
into that difference in actual fact, we falsely
assume that only our particular mate is afflicted with
this sort of weird response to what seems to be a
very simple situation.

For the Christian community, there has been
added an almost awesome and terrifying further confusion. And that is the interpretation of the
book of Ephesians that is used to endorse the idea
that there is a military chain-of-command power
structure in the home. It goes like this: man is
the number one final authority in the home, subject
only to the opinions of God himself; the woman
must submit herself utterly to this authority in
the man, and the children must submit themselves to the father and the mother. If this is true,
it means that a man is obligated to treat his neighbor
better than he treats his wife. He must love
his neighbor as he loves himself. I'm sure that he

wouldn't get very far with his neighbor with that kind of a rigid authoritarian approach, and I'm equally sure the neighbor wouldn't get very far with him if he tried that kind of a dictatorial relationship.

Another insidious thing that is implicit in this sort of an approach to the situation is the idea that the man is somehow superior to the woman. When the Bible says that the woman is the "weaker sex" I don't believe that it has anything to do with man being superior to the woman. It simply means that on an average he is physically stronger than she is.

It isn't that either man or woman is superior to the other; it is simply that we are different. If the Bible would lend to the man any position of greater authority, it would simply be because of the role that God has given him, rather than any idea that he is somehow superior to the woman.

How are we different? Men and women are generally given different roles to fulfill in life. The fact that the woman has the babies automatically establishes different roles to fulfill. In the overview of the Bible, man is given the spiritual responsibility for his wife and children. Moreover, he is to be the provider and protector of his family. "He that provides not for his own has denied the faith and is worse than an infidel."[4] Not only that, but man is to be the fountainhead of love in the home. This is a love which nourishes, cherishes and protects his wife. She is the object of his love.[5] Surely when the Bible spells out the idea that a man is to protect his wife and lovingly care for her as part of his own body, it means that he is psychologically and emotionally protecting her, as well as physically protecting her. This would surely mean that the favorite practice of some husbands in making their wives the butt of their jokes and the object of veiled ridicule would be utterly inconsistent with loving her as Christ loved the Church.

Paul says, "The love of Christ constrains us."[6] As I see it, there is no way for a husband to demand submission on the part of his wife without violating the command of God for him to be loving. Let the love of Christ in him have that constraining effect on a wife and he may discover that she is no longer rebellious or fearful about the idea of submitting to that kind of leadership in the home.

"You wives must submit to your husband's leadership in the same way you submit to the Lord."[7] There is no suggestion here that a woman submits to a man's leadership because he is superior or she is inferior. As I see it, the only possible reason she should submit to his leadership is because of the awful responsibilities he has in the eyes of God. When we elect a government official to a position of responsibility, we must confer on him the necessary authority to fulfill the responsibility. The same thing is true in the home. It is only because of the responsibility that the man must have the authority. However, since he cannot compel the woman to give him that authority, the only way he will ever get it is for her to confer that authority on him. The reason she should confer that authority on him is that he bears the responsibility that God has laid on his shoulders.

As you may have gathered, there have been times in my life when my actions were not exactly brilliant. One such time took place when, half joking and half serious, I thrust my New Testament under my wife's nose with my finger pointing to the word *submit*. I then said to her, "Would you tell me what that little word *submit*

means?" Quick as a flash, the response I got
was this, "Sub means under, and mit means hand.
It means, don't be underhanded with your wife!"
I still haven't found an adequate come-back
to that one. The wife of a well-known Christian
leader told me one time, with a twinkle in her
eye, "I believe there's a time to submit and I
believe there's a time to outwit!"

Certainly, submission does not mean that the
husband arbitrarily makes his decisions without con-
sultation with his wife. To do so is to deny the
reality of what God intended in giving him his
wife in the first place. He needs her insight on almost every subject in order that he can have
the advantage of her view of things. She is the rest
of what God intended him to be. To come to a decision without really hearing her valuable ideas
on the subject is like declaring the results of an
election when you haven't received word from half
of the precincts. This does not mean tolerating
the expression of her viewpoint only to go on the
way you had planned originally. It means listening to her as though she were providing you
with the other half of the wisdom that God has in
mind for you in your decision-making.

Naturally, a man can't be expected to call home
and ask his wife's opinion about everything concerning his vocation. That would be absurd. However,
there may be those occasions when, baffled by something confronting him in his vocation, he would
be well advised to consult with her about it. I
would suggest that where there are serious differences, decisions be postponed until the differences
can be better reconciled. Decisions that involve
both husband and wife should constitute an amalgama-
tion of both their viewpoints in order to extract
the best wisdom that God has to offer. If time

demands a decision before those differences can be reconciled, or compromised, then the man has to exercise the best judgment he has and proceed to make the decision, knowing that he bears the responsibility.

Beside the difference in roles that God has given to the husband and the wife, I believe that there are essentially different approaches to life itself. It is interesting that in that much quoted passage from Ephesians, God instructs the husband to love his wife as Christ loves the Church and suggests to the wife that she submit to her husband's leadership in the same way that she submits to Christ. It isn't a submission of compulsion but of election. It isn't a leadership of tyranny but of love. It seems to me that God is saying to the woman that it is reasonable that there can be only one head of a household. The often offered scheme that marriage is a 50-50 proposition simply won't work, any more than it would work in these United States if we allowed two men to be president, with equal powers and equal responsibilities. In practice, what would happen is that one man would order a certain action and the other one would veto it. It's reasonable then that we confer upon one official both the responsibility and the authority.

An amusing example of the situation that would develop in a "50-50" marriage is the law governing rail traffic in one of our southern states. The law says, "Where two railroad tracks intersect the following rules shall govern rights of way. Both trains shall stop and neither shall start until the other has passed."

God's command to the man in reference to the woman zeros in not at the level of reason but the level of emotion. He says that the man should love his wife in the same way that Christ loved the Church and gave himself for it. Interesting, isn't it? To the woman, an appeal to reason, and to the man, an appeal to his emotions. I wonder if God isn't saying to us something that signals another great difference between men and women. Namely, that a man tends to go at life headfirst. He is basically a rational being who wants an orderly thought process and outline by which to reach his conclusions. Could it be then that God's addressing the woman's reason is a suggestion that if the woman is to understand and communicate with her man, she must approach him in a reasonable way.

It is also an observable phenomenon that whereas man tends to approach life headfirst, a woman tends to approach life heartfirst. Could it then be that in God's command to the man to love his wife, he is in effect saying, if you would ever really communicate with and understand this woman, you must move toward her heartfirst. Generally, men want reasons and women want feelings to validate their conclusions. This is not in any way to suggest that a woman isn't a rational creature. It is simply that her intuitive powers predominate in her approach to life. Nor is it to say that a man doesn't have a very definite emotional side of his being. It is simply to say that man generally tends to go toward life in a rational, headfirst way.

Because women tend to be heartfirst, they are also more person-centered. Because they are more person-centered, they are usually more practical, desiring that actions taken have some personal significance or benefit. With man's rational approach he tends to be more theoretical.

I believe it is crucial to note with tremendous emphasis that in no way do I find the man's approach to life better than the woman's. She will be as often right, arriving at conclusions her way, as he will in his. I believe a man has really become a man when he says to himself, "I don't entirely understand how she arrives at her conclusions, but, by gum, I've got to admit she surely is as often right as I am!"

A man's approach to life tends to be vocation-centered, whereas a woman's approach to life tends to be centered in the home and children. I sincerely believe that the need that all wives share in wanting constant reassurances of love from their husbands represents more of a deficiency in the husband than in the wife. She senses that he does not approach life with the heart first as she does. Therefore, intuitively she wants reassurances that he is making adequate compensations for his deficiency.

If a wife shows a lack of interest in a man's vocation, he takes it personally as a lack of interest in himself; whereas the husband who shows a lack of interest in the home, even if it means neglecting to repair a screen or fix a window, is apt to leave his wife with a feeling that he lacks an interest in her. The reason is simply that the home is a projection of herself. No interest in the home means no interest in her.

Others have written with far greater profundity and much more detail on this fascinating subject, and I refer you to their writings.[8] I'm simply hinting at some of the subtle, yet profound, differences between men and women in order to alert us to the significance of these differences. I believe that the difference was designed by God to make for an adventure, seeking oneness and wholeness. But the difference will forever remain a threat if we, like Henry Higgins in *My Fair Lady,* continue to sing, "Why isn't a woman just like a man. . . ?"

Or from the female view, "Why isn't a man just like a woman?"

One cause of unrelieved stress in marriage is the matter of expecting too much from one's mate. Most of us get married with the super-romantic idea that the other person is thereby put in charge of our happiness. This is idolatry in one of its worst forms, and it is to confer on another human being the responsibility which only God should be given. We should be responsive to each other's needs, but stop short of being responsible for the ultimate happiness of our mate.

Both husbands and wives have pampered or spoiled their mates and still left them far short of happiness. If I make my wife responsible for my happiness, then I blame her for my unhappiness. The truth of the matter is that I have been responsible for most of my own unhappiness. Of course, it took me a long time to get to that point where I could see how unfairly I had dealt with her in this regard. I can and should expect her to be responsive to my needs, but in no way hold her responsible, in an ultimate sense, for my happiness. Neither should she hold me responsible for her ultimate happiness, yet she can expect my responsiveness to her needs.[9]

Another source of tremendous communication difficulty for me was a defensiveness which I developed due to my own insecurity. An insecure person cannot tolerate the suggestion that he may be wrong. A contrary idea is always a threat because it suggests the possibility that your idea may not exactly have dropped from Heaven. When I see that the ideas my wife offers are to give me a well-rounded viewpoint, I am much more able really to hear her and find ways to incorporate her insights into a comprehensive understanding.

I have tried to give up entirely even thinking about whether or not my wife is being submissive to me. I've got my hands full trying to determine whether or not I'm truly loving her "as Christ loved the Church and gave himself for it." Since love never compels, my concern is to evidence a love that constrains. Only she can confer upon me the authority of leadership in the home. Life can be so much more pleasant when I see her as a complement and not competition. She is a gift from God to fulfill what is missing in me. This I know: only the Holy Spirit indwelling both of us can give us the power to love or submit. Just before God tells the wives to submit to their husbands, he says, "Honor Christ by submitting to each other."[10] There have been times when the wisdom that God has given my wife was so much superior to my own that I gladly submitted to her viewpoint in place of mine. Even so, I feel as if I'm just on the edge of beginning to learn all that this means. Saying is so much easier than doing. I find that I have daily to make a determination about these things or I easily slip back into my old patterns.

When growing up in southern Mississippi, I was the youngest of three boys. One was six years older than I and the other four years older. I still remember the discouragement I felt when I realized there was no way for me to catch up to them in age. We had a practice in our home that was common to that day. My Mom and Dad use to put a book on our heads in a certain doorjamb in the house, measure our height, and mark it on the doorjamb. In my eagerness to see if I had grown, I would frequently return to the doorjamb and remeasure myself. In those days I kept wondering "how come it's taking me so long to get bigger." Nowadays I wonder how come it's taking me so long to get *better*.

Like many, now I wish I weren't quite so big.

Mark it up to Christian pride, peculiar to Christian men—or perhaps just to me—but I found it very difficult to bring myself to the point of admitting that I needed to get outside help. My needs finally pushed me to seek help from professional counselors. I have discovered that out of one hundred couples in trouble, there will be ninety-five women for every five men eager to get outside help.

Then I discovered another peculiar "hitch-in-my-git-along." There was a great gap between the insights that came to me through counseling and being able to implement those insights in practical ways inside the bonds of matrimony. Food that is not eaten cannot possibly give you energy, and insights that are not implemented in life cannot possibly give you help. Just knowing a thing only serves to cause more frustration when you don't do it. Perhaps I'm slower than most, but even now I'm just beginning to implement some of the things that I learned four and five years ago. I surely don't recommend that long a delay!

I have learned that too much introspection can really lead to morbidity instead of health. When the monastic movement began about midway in church history, there developed a group known as the Hesychastic monks. They sat up on tall pillars and spent their days in endless contemplation of their own navels. Their modern equivalent is found in those people who are always involved in introspection about every aspect of their lives and human relationships. When one becomes that inward, almost no health can develop in any relationship. Everything becomes too sensitive. There has to be a happy balance of healthy outward activities and an acceptance of God's forgiveness in order to be able to endure much in the way of introspection.

What I have offered here are generalizations that apply to most men and women. There will be women with certain more masculine tendencies for whom these generalizations will not fit. Similarly, there will be men with certain feminine tendencies for whom these will seem unsuitable. (Nor do I have homosexual extremes in mind in their cases.) Generally, however, I think you'll find that these insights do apply.

14

Although We Continue to Be in the Battle, the War Has Already Been Won!

IT MAY WELL BE ASKED, "If the Christian life is the kind of struggle and internal warfare that you say it is, and if there is so much pain associated in dying to self, why even bother?" The answer is simple. Though the battles are a struggle, we know that the war has already been won. There's no chance that we can lose. Victory is sure and an accomplished fact. Moreover, right here while the struggle is going on, we do know the joy and love and peace and mercy and grace in that area of our lives that has come under the domination of the Holy Spirit.

Part of coming to reasonable maturity is discovering the truth so succinctly put by a friend of mine. He was a fairly new Christian and had come under the influence of his non-Christian friends, and while on a fishing trip had gotten pretty smashed on beer. When he arrived home in that condition, his wife took one look at him and locked him out and then phoned me. When I arrived, he was sound asleep in the back seat of his automobile. I drove him to the nearest motel, picked him up in my arms and carried him in and put him to bed. Just as I was brushing the sand off his feet, he woke up long enough to see his pastor cleaning him up for beddy-bye time. With a groan he plunged his head in the pillow saying, "Oh, no!"

The next day I went to see him. When it became apparent to him that in no way was I there to excoriate him for his misbehavior, he asked why. I said to him, "Because your conscience has been worked on by an expert, the Holy Spirit! You don't need any further punishment than what you've already given yourself. What you need now is to know that God has forgiven you, and today is the beginning of a whole new life for you."

He looked at me in relieved bewilderment, and made this classic statement, "I know I'm not what the Lord wants me to be, and I suspect I'm not what you want me to be, but I think you will both rejoice in the fact that you've taken all of the fun out of sin for me!"

When we come to that point in our lives, we begin to really know whose side we're on and begin to despise sin in ourselves. It's a struggle, but we can face what we really are because we know that victory is sure. The war has been won. It's hard to top this for an exciting announcement of that victory: "You were dead in sins, and your sinful desires were not yet cut away. Then he gave you a share in the very life of Christ for he forgave all your sins, and blotted out the charges proved against you, the list of his commandments which you have not obeyed. He took this list of sins and destroyed it by nailing it to Christ's cross. In this way God took away Satan's power to accuse you of sin, and God openly displayed to the whole world Christ's triumph at the cross where your sins were all taken away."[1]

Sure, we still have to face physical death, and for a reason: "Yet, even though Christ lives within you, your body will die because of sin; but your spirit will live for Christ has pardoned it."[2] The final obliteration of the last vestige of sin in your enemy-held island is accomplished by that physical death. But your spirit will live because Christ has pardoned it. You see, the sting has been taken out of that physical death because, "Death is swallowed up in victory. O death, where then is your victory? Where then your sting? For sin—the sting that causes death—will all be gone; and the law, which reveals our sins, will no longer be our judge. How we thank God for all this! It is he who makes us victorious through Jesus Christ our Lord! So, my dear brothers, since future victory is sure, be strong and steady, always abounding in the Lord's work, for you know that nothing you do for the Lord is ever wasted as it would be if there were no resurrection."[3]

This is why we can face that enemy-held part of our island with fearlessness. We know what's up ahead. We know already that the devil is the defeated enemy because of Calvary's cross. It's hard to beat this combination. What a combination! "The battle is the Lord's."[4] And we already know who has won the war. Even though you may be looking at a tiny beachhead in your life occupied by the Spirit of God, yet the promise is most certainly yours as it is to the most mature believer that between you and that heavenly future is the promised presence of Jesus Christ all the way. "And he guarantees right up to the end that you will be counted free from all sin and guilt on that day when he returns. God will surely do this for you, for he always does just what he says, and he is the one who invited you into this wonderful friendship with his Son, even Christ our Lord."[5]

With this kind of security, plus the knowledge of total forgiveness and Heaven assured, a question may be forming in the minds of some. It might go like this: "Well, if a person knows that he's already forgiven and has Heaven made, what's to keep him from going out and living any way he wants to?" I want to answer that by telling you a true story that happened to me.

I was conducting my first evangelistic meeting in a little country church in South Carolina. I gave an invitation for people to come and receive Jesus Christ one night, and about six people came forward, among them a little boy twelve years old. He was barefooted and poorly dressed. Later the pastor told me that his mother was in a mental institution and his father was a hopeless alcoholic. In counseling with the lad, I said to him, "Son, are your sins forgiven now that you have received Jesus?"

"Yes, sir," he said.

"How do you know they are forgiven, son?"

"Because the Lord Jesus died for all my sins," was his response.

"You mean your past sins are forgiven?" I queried. "What about your present sins, are they forgiven?"

"Yes, sir, they're forgiven too."

Then I asked, "Well, son, you know that you're not going to be perfect when you walk out of here. What about your future sins? Are they forgiven too?"

"Yes, sir. They're forgiven too," he said.

"Well, then, if that's the case, what's to keep you from walking out of here and living like the devil?" I asked.

His response was classic. He said, "Well, sir, the way I figure it, it was my sins what nailed him to the cross in the first place. And I don't want to cause him no more trouble than I already have."

You see, the boy's heart, now invaded by the Holy Spirit, was expressing the gratitude that a true believer knows, as well as the motivation that anyone has who has seen what it cost God to forgive him. The remembrance of that kind of love can overpower strong temptation.

With that kind of victory assured and that kind of Presence guaranteed, we can now face up to a very important matter.

It has seemed to me in my Christian life that

I reached a certain stage of spiritual growth and literally longed and ached for more of God. I had a real God-hunger that led me to throw myself at almost any potential deepening experience of the Spirit of God. In spite of my efforts in this direction, the God-hunger remained. I since have come to see something I feel is very important. We can only go so far in our spiritual maturation process in seeking to know and receive the blessing of God directly from God himself. It is almost as though he brings us to a certain point and then steps back and says, "Dear, dear children, how brief are these moments before I must go away and leave you! Then, though you search for me, you cannot come to me. . . .and so I am giving a new commandment to you now— *love each other* just as much as I love you. *Your strong love for each other* will prove to the world that you are my disciples."[6]

When we focus on obtaining the power and affirmation of Christ exclusively from Christ himself we're overlooking the crucial horizontal relationships of love through which he always intended that we should both give and receive him and his love. "He that receiveth you, receiveth me."[7] I began to get that additional dimension that I longed for when I decided I would look for him in other people in whom he dwelt. The more I affirmed his presence in them, the more certainly I knew his presence and power in myself in a new and mysterious way. Since this is a rather new thing for me, I can only say that I'm tiptoeing on the edge of a brand new understanding of what it is to love my neighbor as I love myself. "Love the Lord your God with all your heart, soul and mind. This is the first and greatest commandment. The second most important is similar: Love your neighbor as much as you love yourself."[8]

This means that in order to learn to love my neighbor I have to learn what it is to really love myself. This is much easier said than done. What does the Bible teach about self-love? Well, as I see it, the essential nature of the love of God is found in Romans 5:8, "But God commendeth his love toward us in that while we were yet sinners, Christ died for us."[9] God's love is the kind of love that accepted me as I was, even when my behavior was reprehensible in the eyes of God. He didn't approve of my behavior, but he loved me and accepted me as I really was in spite of it.

As a prisoner once put it in a letter to me from jail, "Finally, as I see it, God doesn't change me in order to love me. He loves me in order to change me!" Love, then, is God accepting me just exactly as I am. That loving acceptance is, along with the Holy Spirit, the motivating power that gives me what I need to change my behavior. I no longer have to pretend to be something I'm not. Because of my security in the finished work of Jesus Christ I can be boldly honest about who I am and what I am like. I can face both my vices and my virtues. I can esteem the virtues and set about, by the mercy and power of God, to see his Spirit change the vices.

To love someone else, then, is to accept him as he is and not constantly be laying upon him a demand to change. It is this acceptance of the other person that begins to loosen up the channels of communication so that people can really reveal themselves to others and know others at the same level of self-revelation. My problem has always been a fear that if I really let you know what I am like, you wouldn't like me at all, much less love me. Consequently, most of us wear masks in order that people would not know exactly who we are. For that reason, we oftentimes pretend to be what we really are not.

The three leading psychologists who helped lead the way into today's helpful psychological disciplines were Freud, Jung, and Adler. Freud said man's greatest need was to be loved. Jung said man's greatest need was for security. Adler said that the greatest need of man was for significance. Interesting, that! Because it is usually in the pursuit of one of those three things that we put on a mask of pretense.

The other day I heard Keith Miller say, "Even if you really loved me, I probably won't believe it because I haven't really let you know who I am."[10] I'm not sure of your love unless I have shown the real me to you. This is often what causes one of the startling traps in romance and marriage. A guy sees a gal go bouncing by and says to himself, "Wow! I want that!" He knows that if he lets her know the very basic thing that he wants from her, she'll have nothing to do with him. So he's got to put on a mask. He puts his very best foot forward as the little gentleman, and begins to become to her the kind of person he feels she will respond to. It may not come anywhere close to resembling the real person inside. If she is attracted to him, the chances are she too will put her best foot forward and slip on a mask that she is sure will get a ring on her finger. After they are married and the masks begin to slip, each sees a stranger emerging from behind the countenance of the person they thought they knew well enough to marry.

In the pursuit of significance or in the pursuit of security we are apt to be outwardly what we must be in order to gain these goals. We pretend for so long that we lose touch with who we really are. Nathaniel Hawthorne once said, "No man can for any considerable time, wear one face to himself, and another to the multitude, without finally getting bewildered as to which is the true one."[11]

I'm not proposing that we indiscriminately rip our masks off and traumatize ourselves and everybody else by startling revelations. What I am suggesting is the possibility that we begin to search for that person who can be trusted to receive with Christian love our progressive revelation of self. I can bear this and he can bear this only when we are both operating on the basis of the security that is the gift of every believer in Jesus Christ.

There are two kinds of loneliness that grip us human beings. The first is an existential inner loneliness that only the Holy Spirit of God can fill in our lives. The second kind of loneliness is for another human being with whom we can have deep and honest relationships. Frequently, we get these things confused and look for some person to be to us what only God can be. If I'm hungry, it's no good to show me a steak dinner unless I can put the steak where the hunger is, inside of me. Our loneliness for God can only be alleviated when we are invaded by the Holy Spirit, and receive inner assurance of his perpetual companionship.

Just as frequently, we are looking for God to be to us what he always intended that another human being should be. Many are looking for manifestations of God in their own experience that would call for another incarnation on the part of Jesus. We will see him again, but not until the second coming. Until then he fully intended that each of us should be some reflection of his present incarnation in us, so that we could visibly manifest to one another that love and care, affirmation and concern that he desires that we sense from him.

Completeness of personality is our goal, becoming a well-rounded whole person manifesting at least in some vague reflection all of the aspects of the marvelous personality of Jesus. Perhaps the aspiration of trying to be like Jesus Christ is just too lofty to contemplate. But the Apostle Paul was a regulation flesh and blood human being. His life is an example for all—for you and for me and for all others who will come to believe in Jesus Christ. And his life showed a healthy, strong, vertical relationship with God, and deep, abiding, and honest relationships with his friends. One has but to count the number of personal names mentioned in the 16th chapter of Romans to realize how deeply involved he was with other persons. Paul had it all. It took lots and lots of time. But as long as God gives us the time and shows us his unlimited patience, dare we settle for less than that completeness of personality which is the essence of maturity?

NOTES

CHAPTER ONE
1. 2 Corinthians 5:17 (KJV).
2. Galatians 5:22, 23a.

CHAPTER TWO
1. Revelation 3:20 (KJV).
2. John 14:17 (*The Living Bible*); Galatians 2:20 (TLB); 1 Corinthians 6:19 (TLB).
3. John 14:15, 16 (TLB).

CHAPTER THREE
1. Romans 7:15, *New Testament in Modern English* by J. B. Phillips. The MacMillan Co., New York, New York.
2. Isaiah 59:2, RSV, *Harper Study Bible*, Zondervan Publishing House, Grand Rapids, Michigan.
3. Revelation 3:20 (KJV).

CHAPTER FIVE
1. Hebrews 10:14 (TLB).
2. 1 Corinthians 1:8, 9 (TLB).
3. Mairet, Phillip. *Christian Essays in Psychology.* Published by Philosophical Library, New York, p. 61.
4. Ibid., p. 41.
5. Loc. cit.
6. Romans 7:15 (Phillips).
7. Hebrews 4:12 (TLB).
8. Hebrews 4:13 (TLB).
9. Romans 7:18 (TLB).
10. 1 Timothy 1:15, *The Holy Bible, Berkeley Version in Modern English*, Zondervan Publishing House.
11. Romans 7:23, 24 (Phillips).
12. Psalm 103:13, 14 (Berkeley).

CHAPTER SIX
1. John 15:3 (KJV).
2. 1 John 1:8, 9 (KJV).
3. 1 John 2:1 (KJV).
4. A portion of Chapter 6 appeared originally in *Decision* magazine as an article by Lane Adams entitled "Care of Newborn Christians." It was later reprinted as a pamphlet. This material is copyrighted © 1966 by the Billy Graham Evangelistic Association, and is adapted for use in this book with the permission of the Association.

CHAPTER SEVEN
1. Matthew 9:17 (TLB).
2. From a message delivered at the U.S. Congress on Evangelism in Minneapolis, Minnesota, 1966.
3. Philippians 3:11-14 (TLB).
4. Jeremiah 17:9 (Berkeley).
5. Mark 7:20-23 (Berkeley).

CHAPTER EIGHT
1. Matthew 6:33 (KJV).
2. Galatians 5:16, 17 (TLB).
3. Galatians 5:19-21 (TLB).
4. Romans 6:16 (TLB).
5. Colossians 2:16, 17, 20–23 (TLB).
6. John 13:35 (KJV).
7. John 13:17 (KJV).
8. Ecclesiastes 1:17, 18 (Berkeley).
9. Colossians 2:18, 19 (TLB).
10. 2 Corinthians 5:7 (Berkeley).
11. Luke 6:31 (KJV).
12. John 13:17 (KJV).
13. Matthew 4:4 (KJV).

CHAPTER NINE
1. 1 Timothy 1:15, 16 (Berkeley).
2. Galatians 1:16, 17 (Berkeley).
3. Galatians 1:18-20 (Berkeley).
4. Acts 9:23-25 (Berkeley).
5. Acts 9:26 (Berkeley).
6. Acts 9:30 (Berkeley).
7. Galatians 1:21-23 (Berkeley).
8. Acts 9:31 (Berkeley).
9. Acts 11:30.

10. Acts 13:2-4 (Berkeley).
11. 1 Timothy 5:22 (Berkeley).
12. Haywood, John. Proverbs, Part 1, Chapter 2, *Familiar Quotations by John Bartlett,* (Little and Brown).
13. 1 Thessalonians 2:7, 8 (TLB).
14. 1 Thessalonians 4:18 (TLB).
15. Matthew 4:4 and 1 Peter 2:2.
16. 1 Timothy 4:7, 8.
17. Longfellow, Henry Wadsworth. *The Courtship of Miles Standish, Familiar Quotations by John Bartlett* (Little and Brown).

CHAPTER TEN
1. 1 Timothy 5:22 (KJV).

CHAPTER ELEVEN
1. *Webster's Seventh New Collegiate Dictionary* (Springfield: G. & C. Merriam Company).
2. 1 John 1:8—2:2 (TLB).

CHAPTER TWELVE
1. John 13:35 (KJV).
2. Galatians 5:22, 23a *New American Standard Version*
3. 1 Corinthians 12:31 (KJV).
4. 1 Corinthians 13:3 (NASB).
5. Hebrews 2:4 (TLB).
6. Ephesians 4:13 (Berkeley).
7. 1 John 1:9 (KJV).
8. 1 Timothy 1:16 (Berkeley).
9. Ephesians 4:13 (Berkeley).
10. 1 Thessalonians 2:7, 8 (TLB).
11. Romans 8:29 (KJV).

CHAPTER THIRTEEN
1. Psalm 101:2 (TLB).
2. Genesis 2:18 (Berkeley).
3. Founder and president of the American Institute of Family Relations, 5287 Sunset Blvd., Hollywood, California. From a newspaper column, date unknown.
4. 1 Timothy 5:8 (KJV).
5. Ephesians 5:23-33 (TLB).
6. 2 Corinthians 5:14 (KJV).
7. Ephesians 5:22 (TLB).
8. Cecil Osborne, *The Art of Understanding Your Mate,* Zondervan; and Paul Tournier, *To Understand Each Other,* John Knox Press.
9. For this and many other insights I am in the debt of Dr. John Narciso, professor of psychology, Trinity University, San Antonio, Texas.
10. Ephesians 5:21 (TLB).

CHAPTER FOURTEEN
1. Colossians 2:13-15 (TLB).
2. Romans 8:10 (TLB).
3. 1 Corinthians 15:54-58 (TLB).
4. 1 Samuel 17:47 (KJV).
5. 1 Corinthians 1:8, 9 (TLB).
6. John 13:33-35 (TLB).
7. Matthew 10:40 and John 13:20 (KJV).
8. Matthew 22:37-39 (TLB).
9. Romans 5:8 (KJV).
10. From a message delivered at the Celebration of New Life, First Presbyterian Church of Hollywood, California, February 1975.
11. Quoted by Robert J. McCracken in a sermon on the radio broadcast, "National Radio Pulpit."